ACCUSED OF WITCHCRAFT
᪣ IN ᪣
NEW YORK

ACCUSED OF WITCHCRAFT IN NEW YORK

S·R· FERRARA

THE
History
PRESS

Published by The History Press
Charleston, SC
www.historypress.com

First published 2023

Manufactured in the United States

ISBN 9781467153515

Library of Congress Control Number: 2022947162

Notice: The information in this book is true and complete to the best of our knowledge. It is offered without guarantee on the part of the author or The History Press. The author and The History Press disclaim all liability in connection with the use of this book.

To Tara and Scout

CONTENTS

PREFACE

I have this childhood memory from when my grandfather accidentally left a jigsaw puzzle out in the rain. The pieces were completely soggy, wet and limp, and he tried to fix the puzzle by laying the individual pieces to dry indoors. I remember playing with some of the soggier pieces and attempting to fit them together. Some were too damaged and deteriorated to ever be used accurately again, but still my grandfather attempted to fix and complete the puzzle, as stubborn and unrelentless as he was. In many ways, this memory reminds me of the pursuit of historical research. Those who came before you have already begun to dry the individual, damp pieces, or moments of history, to construct some corner of a puzzle, a reconstruction of some past circumstance. Some pieces of history are just too damaged and possibly lost forever (or at least too mangled to be used accurately). And you, the one who is just now approaching this puzzle, the best you can do is identify pieces, work on them to dry them out and return form to them, interpret them if you will and figure out how they fit into the bigger picture. That is what I hope to do with this book. My research into witchcraft accusations is not a complete understanding of the past but rather an attempt to identify and interpret these historical jigsaw puzzle pieces in hopes that others may use this text to further add to a bigger picture.

I've been interested in witchcraft for as long as I could remember but found difficulty in learning about the witches from my own state of New York. Specifically, I wanted to know if I lived nearby some historical witch's home that I could go visit. Unfortunately, no such book existed that could point me in the right direction. Instead, I have relied on brief testimonies within state and local archives, chapters from witchcraft histories, small tidbits of information from genealogies, newspaper clippings, local folklore, local historians and footnotes in historical texts. Along my research journey, I even found out that my own family lineage, nine generations back, had a direct connection to this social phenomenon: the Lyon family (on my paternal grandmother's side) gave testimony during the trial of Goody Knapp and Goody Staples in Fairfield, Connecticut. These personal connections seemed to only emotionally connect me more to the study of witchcraft history.

I've brought these historical references together in one place to provide likewise enthusiasts and researchers with one location to learn the stories of individuals accused of witchcraft in the state of New York. However, researching and writing wasn't quite satisfying enough for me, and I was compelled to go visit some of these locations mentioned in my book. In January 2021, my wife, Tara, and I embarked on a New York road trip, stopping at numerous locations within eastern New York to visit historical sites, shrines and graveyards where some of the accused in New York history resided. I've found that there is something rather *Scooby Doo* about researching witches. You get interested by the magic and the spooky monstrous themes, but by the end of your research, you find out it's the very real and familiar community members who are the true monsters for their spiteful accusations and the person standing at the end of all the different accusatory pointed fingers is really the innocent one. It is my hope that you find this book interesting, informative and inspiring enough to leave your home and go visit some of the historic locations mentioned within and pause to reflect on the lived experiences of all those who walked there before you. Also, please keep in mind that these historical accounts are but one aspect to a much broader past of American history. I encourage you to not only visit the spaces with which these witchcraft accusation victims were associated but also stop by the local historical societies and museums and learn more about the social environments in which these people lived.

ACKNOWLEDGEMENTS

There were a few research and literary obstacles to avoid while writing this book, and it's necessary to thank those who were helpful in this endeavor. I began researching witchcraft accounts nearly a decade ago, and the first compiled list of accused individuals I came across was in an internet database curated by scholar Marc Carlson, director of Special Collections at the McFarlin Library of the University of Tulsa. His publicly accessible research proved to be a treasure-trove of academic writings, compiled lists of historic individuals accused of witchcraft throughout the world and a vast array of his other research projects. His research was invaluable to this book, and when I was ready to publish, I attempted to reach out to Marc and introduce myself, only to find his website domain expired and unfortunately hear of his recent passing. Even though we never met, thank you, Marc, for being an inspiration. Public accessibility of research matters.

That being said, I should also thank the New Netherland Institute, New York Public Library, Hathi Trust Digital Library and other institutions for their public and free online databases that are truly invaluable to scholars.

Thank you to Islip Town historian George Munkenbeck, Maureen Folk of the Glen Falls Chapman Museum, the Office of Staten Island borough president Vito J. Fossella and the Three Village Historical Society for all of your help. I also thank all of the hard work from The History Press team who worked to make this book possible, especially my editors J. Banks Smither and Abigail Fleming. I truly appreciate all your hard work.

Lastly, thank you to my wife, friends and family who were all very supportive of this project; who read and critiqued earlier versions of this book; and who endured hours of sobering history facts while attempting to enjoy a nice night out on the town free of serious discussion. I love you all.

INTRODUCTION

T his book focuses on the individuals accused of witchcraft in New York, or rather areas within the borders of New York State at present. This distinction is made because the phenomenon of witchcraft accusations predates the state of New York as it is currently known. The accounts provided in this text are focused biographical narratives not intended to be a detailed and intensive examination of each individual's life but rather the period of each person's life when they were accused or suspected of witchcraft as well as the appropriate context needed. Through my research, I have compiled the biographical accounts of thirty individuals accused or suspected of witchcraft throughout two centuries of New York State history. These accounts offer insights into community belief systems and the horrors one could face when targeted as a witch. But first, what do we mean by the term *witch*?

In today's popular culture, we accept that witches can be nice and benefit the community. In fact, New Age spiritual movements like Wicca have reclaimed the terms *witch* and *witchcraft* in an effort to honor the victims of Early Modern state-sponsored executions, particularly European women healers. But one doesn't need to be a Wiccan in today's age to consider themselves witchy. Maybe they are herbal healers, midwives, psychics, spiritual guides, nature lovers, social media influencers or perhaps just avid Harry Potter fans who take J.K. Rowling's universe far too seriously. The word *witch*, for most of history, has evoked the notions of harm and malevolence—think of a Harry Potter world of just Voldemorts and

Above: Map of accused witches in New York State. Stars represent clusters of individuals accused of witchcraft that resided in New York. *Courtesy of author.*

Opposite: Faust's pact with Mephisto after Goethe's *Faust*, engraving (1840). *Wikimedia Commons / Public domain.*

muggles. Anthropologist E.E. Evans-Pritchard defined witchcraft as the "inherited ability to cause misfortune or death."[1] Witches were not healers; they were strictly a force to be reckoned with, feared and avoided. Those accused of witchcraft—such as healers, midwives, clergymen, prostitutes and paupers—all performed a role within society (whether given or forced into), and no one intentionally took up the position of "town witch," unless to intentionally invoke fear. Rather, the role of witch was assigned to a person through accusation as a way to explain misfortune and cast blame onto an individual who could then be held responsible for intentionally causing a harmful event. There were two types of witchcraft people could be accused of practicing in colonial America: *maleficium* and diabolical.[2] Often an accusation of witchcraft included both maleficium and diabolical evidence. *Maleficium* is a Latin term meaning "harmful sorcery" and is used to describe a negative spiritual force that a witch exerts to cause harm to a person's health or property. Diabolical witchcraft is more concerned with the origin of these powers and describes evil supernatural abilities that were bestowed on a witch by a direct pact with the devil. This is often seen

in testimonies or forced confessions of an accused individual, that they had signed their name in the "devil's book." In the seventeenth century, books were luxury items that signaled power, wealth and education, all of which were not afforded to most people. For the pious, the voice of God was contained within a book (the Bible), and it was only fitting the devil had his own book. However, the devil's book contained the names of the souls he commanded.

There is a common misconception that the fear of witchcraft was culturally and temporally localized to White Europeans in the seventeenth century. Respectfully, this makes sense to those with only a casual interest in the subject. After all, the Salem Witch Trials of 1692–93 were a pivotal event in U.S. history and commonly taught in primary schools across the nation as a lesson in hysteria, wrongful conviction and the mayhem caused by religious zealots in positions of political authority. We are told that European settlers in Salem, Massachusetts, lost trust in one another and began to accuse people of bewitchment, thereby leading to a frenzy of legal trials, imprisonment and executions. However, we are not told that the fear of witchcraft was not localized to Salem or even to White people. In fact, historians and archaeologists have observed this particular fear in Europeans, Native Americans and enslaved Africans, permeating all of the colonies, extending well into the twentieth century. Witchcraft is still feared in contemporary societies throughout the world. For example, the historical (written) record is full of instances where individuals were accused and sometimes executed on the suspicion of witchcraft throughout much of the United States. Archaeologists have also found material evidence of apotropaic items intended to protect the occupants of a house from bewitchment. Items like carved magical symbols, leather shoes, witch bottles, dried feline corpses and horseshoes all served the purpose of spiritual protection to those who feared the repercussions of angering a nearby witch.[3] Today, people employ charms to ward away negative energy and attract good fortune. These charms, each with different cultural histories and meanings from throughout the world, are now entangled in the melting pot we know as New York.

A postcard wishing good luck illustrated by various lucky charms. Chromolithograph. *Wellcome Collection.*

So why then do we not see enslaved African people accused of witchcraft in the history pages of the northeastern United States? In short, we do see instances of Black people accused of witchcraft, they are just seldom discussed. During the age of the Atlantic slave trade, Africans were perceived by Europeans as the lowest class of society and were not considered to have the agency with which to exert spiritual damage to their European enslavers. This is not to say that some Africans were not accused over time, but not nearly as often as Europeans and Native Americans. Further, historians in the past have largely favored European communities when discussing American witchcraft history due to the prevalence of racism in academia, and it wasn't until recent decades that non-White communities in America were recognized and centered in historical writing.

Let's for a brief moment travel to Massachusetts to examine the enslaved individual Tituba of the Salem Witch Trials. It is commonly believed through pop culture that Tituba was Black and one of the first to be accused of witchcraft during the Salem hysteria. However, her race has changed through different historical recordings of the infamous witch trials. In fact, researchers like Chadwick Hansen (1974) found that Tituba was likely Carib Indian from the West Indies and that historians have continually changed her race through time from "Native" to "Half-Native and Half-Black" to "full Black." During the seventeenth century, Europeans would not accept that Africans had the ability or intellectual agency to bewitch their European enslavers; they would, however, accept that a Native American had such power. After all, the European settlers were "facing the devil on two fronts": the witches of the invisible world and the Indians in the visible,[4] having been continually engaged in conflict with the local Indigenous people. It wasn't until after the Civil War that historians begin to identify Tituba as African, given nineteenth-century America was renegotiating slavery and Black identity.[5] Therefore, the changing race of Tituba through the historical record is likely a reflection of the increased European-perceived agency of African Americans and the biases of White historians pushing back, slowly transforming Tituba from Indian to African and implicitly placing blame of the 1692–93 mass hysteria on African Americans. The witchcraft hysteria of Salem also saw the accusation of two enslaved African women, Mary Black and Candy, and although their coerced confessions landed them in jail for a brief period of time, they were released and acquitted.

More so, for much of New York's history, African Americans had been an enslaved people and, through constant struggle for rights and recognition through abolitionist movements, finally gained their freedom in the nineteenth century. However, the road to freedom was gradual, with several progressing policies passed by New York State legislation and constant pushback by White supremacists. In New York, the "Act for the Gradual Abolition of Slavery" was passed in 1799. It granted manumission to children born after July 4 under the condition they serve as indentured servants until the age of twenty-eight for males and twenty-five for females.[6] However, this legislation did not free any currently enslaved people. In 1817, following the War of 1812 and the respected role of African American soldiers, the state was pressured to move further to free all enslaved people born before July 4, 1799, although this policy would not be actionable until 1827. Even then, children born at this cusp would still be subject to the indentured servitude as outlined in the previous policy. These changes in human rights happened rather late in the light of American witchcraft history, and one cannot even imagine what horrors faced enslaved Africans during its height.

However, throughout the seventeenth and eighteenth centuries of New York State history, there are no instances of enslaved or manumitted African people explicitly accused of witchcraft—at least not in the traditional explicit ways. There is one instance in the eighteenth century that may indicate a fear of African spirituality (notably witchcraft) among White Europeans in New York City. In 1741, fires raged in the uninhabited outskirts of New York City, and soon gossip spread that enslaved and manumitted Africans and lower-class White citizens had initiated a secret plot to burn down the city. The rumors soon snowballed into mass panic, which resulted in the execution of eighteen enslaved Africans and four White "co-conspirators" by public hanging in a hysteria that has been compared to the Salem Witch Trials.[7] What's relevant about this event is that eleven other enslaved Africans were executed by judicial immolation, also known as burning at the stake. In the European motherland, burning at the stake was a punishment reserved for those "possessed" by the devil; the burning of a corpse after some other form of execution also indicates a witchcraft crime in European contexts.[8] White New Yorkers feared not only the physical threats from Black people but also spiritual threats, along with the moral threats of enslaved Africans rising up against their White enslavers.[9] Scholars like Timothy McMillan argue that burning to death at the stake sent a clear symbolic message to any future would-be perpetrators that disobedience and physical violence were an affront to not only the White enslavers but also to God as a crime of pure satanic evil.[10]

Gender also plays an important role in the analysis of witchcraft accusations. For example, European history is fraught with religious extremism, especially when discussing women's rights. The term *witch* had been attributed to men and women by Native American communities, and men could be (and were) accused of witchcraft in Euro-American settlements. Regardless, the majority of accused or suspected witches in American history, broadly, were women—a common theme in traditional European witchcraft accusations.

This attribution of witches and femininity can be connected to religious and cultural perspectives and ideas on sexuality and nature. In *Women, Culture, and Society* (1974), Michelle Rosaldo writes,

> *What is perhaps most striking is the fact that cultural notions of the female often gravitate around natural or biological characteristics: fertility, maternity, sex, and menstrual blood. And women, as wives, mothers, witches, midwives, nuns, and whores, are defined almost exclusively in terms of their sexual functions. A witch, in European tradition, is a woman who sleeps with the devil; and a nun is a woman who marries her god. Again, purity and pollution are ideas that apply primarily to women, who must either deny their physical bodies or circumscribe their dangerous sexuality.* [11]

In this passage, Rosaldo is furthering her argument about the problematic perceptions of male and female agencies and roles within society. However, these sentiments reflect seventeenth-century European cultural perspectives. Accused witches back in Europe were mostly women, while court testimonies and lore had an overtly sexual nature to them. These ideas of what witchcraft could be traveled with Europeans into the American frontier. In the colonies, women were not only restricted by puritanical laws and policies but could also find themselves accused of supernatural crimes such as witchcraft.

While European witchcraft is often focused on the feminine and sexuality, American witchcraft (specifically within the confines of New York) may have taken different forms. After all, the multiple cultural and environmental causes for witchcraft accusations in Europe were different than those on the American frontier. The male to female ratio of individuals accused in New York, in total, was 1:2 during the seventeenth and eighteenth centuries. However, this ratio is not a particularly reliable way of viewing witchcraft history, and the reader should be warned against tallying the masculine and feminine names listed in this text. After all, these individuals represent different cultures, contexts and beliefs occupying the same territory. This book does not just focus on those accused individuals of European ancestry of the former Dutch and British colony but also the several sovereign tribal nations that exist within the borders of New York. If we are to examine these ratios closely, we can see that the number of people accused changes not only by century but also by which community accused the suspected witch (European or Native). Ratios, in this case, are proven to be an unreliable way to understand how gender figures into the broad patterns of this intercultural phenomenon. Native Americans had witchcraft accusers and victims, and their cultures were different from the English, who also dealt with witchcraft accusers and victims, and were different than the Dutch, who were different from the multiple African and Caribbean cultures all entangled in early New York. Of course, it's much easier to isolate one cultural group and examine a phenomenon like witchcraft within an established research scope, but this fails to acknowledge the entanglement of cultures represented in New York and the process of colonialism in America. The particularities and context of each witchcraft accusation are more crucial to understanding the relationship between gender and witchcraft. Frankly, it is important to understand that different cultures had different motivations to accuse an individual of witchcraft.

Ultimately, the question boils down to, What can we truly gain from a focused study of witchcraft in New York and how witchy even is New York? Well, it might surprise most people to hear, but New York is quite the witchy place! In 1966, Raymond Buckland not only introduced the United States to Wicca but also opened the first witchcraft museum in the United States, located in Bay Shore, New York.[12] Today, over one million Americans believe in spiritual forms of witchcraft. Spiritualism, occultism and New Age beliefs also have their roots in New York. In 1848, the infamous Fox Sisters sparked the spiritualism movement in the United States from their family home in Rochester, New York, by popularizing the idea that humans could communicate with the deceased through various forms of conjuring. Focusing on New York is also unique because New Yorkers themselves are unique. As you will read in these biographical narratives, New York has traditionally been a melting pot of cultures and belief systems, as well as a haven for those "huddled masses" seeking not only a new place to call home but also protection from those who would see them hang as witches (such is the case in the Salem Refugees section).

This book has been designed to not only explore the multiple accounts of witchcraft accusation but also investigate and explain the numerous false accounts that have become commonplace stories over time, weaving superstition and historical events into New York folklore. This book briefly dips into the lives of thirty individuals accused of witchcraft as recorded in the written and oral histories of New York. The majority of these accounts include the stories of real individuals, while some accounts, or rather individuals, are purely the invention of local folklore. Folkloric accounts of accused witches have been investigated here with some scrutiny to determine if these fictional accounts allude to some specific individual(s) whose names

The Four Witches by Albrecht Dürer (1497). *Creative Commons.*

may have been lost to history. The following biographies of New York's accused witches are grouped by century in order to follow the historical trajectory and listed in chronological order (as best as could be discerned). Transcriptions of original historical documents have been modernized to help the reader. Lastly, it is important to keep in mind that, although the following accounts may include testimonies of diabolical witchcraft and supernatural attacks, none of the mentioned individuals were actual witches but rather innocent people targeted by their neighbors during heightened times of fear and anxiety.

DATE	NAME	LOCATION	GENDER
1642	Reńe Goupil	Our Lady of Martyrs Shrine, Ossernenon (Auriesville, NY)	M
1642	Isaac Jogues	(see Reńe Goupil)	M
1646	John de Lalande	(see Reńe Goupil)	M
1650	Sachem Poggatacut	Suffolk County, NY	M
1652	Cornelis Melyn	Staten Island, NY	M
1656	Sachem Wyandanch	Suffolk County, NY	M
1658	Elizabeth Garlick	East Hampton, NY	F
1660	Mary Wright Andrews	Oyster Bay, NY	F
1662	Judith (Varleth) Bayard	Manhattan, NY	F
1662	Goodwife Ayres	New York (Unidentified)	F
1665	Mary Hall	Setauket, NY	F
1665	Ralph Hall	Setauket, NY	M
1670	Katherine Harrison	Westchester Square, Bronx	F
1681	Maes Cornelis	Albany, NY	M
1683	Hannah Travally	Southampton, NY	F
1692	Goodwife Miller	Bedford, NY	F
1692	Philip English	Salem, MA/NYC	M
1692	Mary English	Salem, MA/NYC	F

Date	Name	Location	Gender
1692	Elizabeth Cary	Salem, MA/NYC	F
1692	Winifred King Benham	Staten Island, NY	F
1692	Winifred Benham Junior	Staten Island, NY	F
1700	Unnamed Woman No. 1/Bewitcher of Aquendero's Son	Albany, NY	F
1710–20	Unnamed Woman No. 2	Staten Island, NY	F
1727	Aunty Greenleaf	Brookhaven, NY	F
1730	Buckinjehillish	Seneca Nation	M
1735	Mary Newton	Oakdale, NY	F
1758	Mary Jemison	Seneca Nation	F
1777	Margaret Telford	Salem, NY	F
1799	Unnamed Woman No. 3	Seneca Nation	F
Late eighteenth century	Nancy Juson	Lambert's Lane, Staten Island, NY	F

I
SEVENTEENTH CENTURY

Look out for the old woman
with the wart on her nose
what she'll do to yer
nobody knows
for she knows the devil

—*"Hist Whist" by e.e. cummings (Tulips and Chimneys, 1923)*

1

INTRODUCTION TO THE
SEVENTEENTH CENTURY

The seventeenth century in the United States is a difficult time to study. After all, we are taught in school that this colonial period marked our society's earliest allochthonous communities, and the struggles endured way back then helped to build a nation. It is a time taught to us of "pilgrims and Indians," quiet village streets and simple yet arduous daily tasks. We think of this period as one of discipline to authority, extreme piousness to the Christian God and the toils of life at the frontier of empires. This view of history is not the full picture. First, our histories tend to center the experiences of European settlers, all while reducing Indigenous and African people to mere elements of the backdrop. Also, we seldomly discuss the consequences of ruminating gossip within communities and how on occasion those petty rumors would snowball into accusations of occult crime and circumstances of pure horror entangled in the stressors of a highly kinetic environment.

In many ways, this book is a collection of horror stories, at least for those who had to experience betrayal and accusation from their neighbors. Most of these events are true, although some are folklore, and center on the lives of individuals or families. To be clear, this text primarily draws on the written record of people accused of witchcraft after the arrival of Europeans in America. Native Americans, such as the Iroquois and Algonquian people, inhabited the region we now call New York for thousands of years before Europeans and had a belief system that sometimes attributed the causation of harmful events to maleficent supernatural forces. However, the belief in witchcraft and the subsequent accusation of individuals suspected of witchcraft saw a rise after European contact and the spread of the Christian belief systems.[13] The biblical devil arrived in the Americas with the early European settler, and the spread of European belief systems began an era of diabolical witchcraft throughout North and South America.

The belief in witches dates back to pre-Roman times and has taken on several different forms throughout the centuries. This book is focused on the most modern form, that of diabolical witchcraft, or rather, witchcraft as an evil power gained by a deal with the Christian devil. The story of New York witchcraft begins in England more than two hundred years before the colonization of New York. During this time, English laws directly addressed the intense fear of witches living within communities and wreaking havoc. There were many historical villains who capitalized on this hysteria and perpetuated this fear for self gain. In 1484, a papal bull[14] titled *Summis desiderantes affectibus*[15] was issued by Pope Innocent VIII and sought the widespread persecution of those suspected of witchcraft, a crime punishable by death.[16] Although the Catholic Church and England were separated during the English Reformation of the fifteenth century, this decree was still influential on the people of England. Their fear of witches was now validated by the highest authority. This decree was further perpetuated by Heinrich Kramer publishing the notorious *Malleus Maleficarum*[17] (1486), which outlined how to identify, prosecute and execute convicted witches.[18] The *Malleus Maleficarum* soon became the playbook used by many colonial authorities during the trial of suspected witches. Witch paranoia gained momentum throughout Europe and saw its peak between 1560 and 1630.[19] As the hysteria in Europe began to calm after the 1630s, the fringes of the British empire in North America continued to suspect, try and convict hundreds of people for the crime of witchcraft.

King James VI, known for uniting the Scottish and English crowns under one monarch, was particularly interested in the supernatural, as demonstrated by his work *Daemonologie*[20] (1597), which discussed modern necromancy and black magic. King James's work marked a height in witchcraft paranoia, as it was a text validating witchcraft fears, written by a sitting monarch, and likely inspired and empowered local authorities to prosecute and execute those suspected of witchcraft.

Paranoia about witchcraft was widespread through Europe from the fifteenth to the seventeenth century and contributed to the identity of European culture. Supernatural explanations for misfortune and the subsequent fear of the occult traveled with Europeans to the Americas as a part of European heritage. Life abroad, be it in North or South America, involved many new difficulties to daily life and challenges to individual—and family—identity. The persecution of witches gripped Europe for nearly two centuries before colonization of eastern North America and surely would have persisted in some form as a part of European identity and heritage among the early settlers crossing the Atlantic during this period.

The process of European colonialism in northeastern North America affected not only the European settlers but also Native American groups, like the Algonquian, and enslaved African people. The term *Algonquian* refers to the large group of Native Americans who occupied much of the eastern coast of North America and spoke variations of the Algonquian language. The belief in witchcraft was mutual among the European settlers, the Algonquians and Africans. In fact, the European proselytization of the Algonquians included the spiritual beliefs of witchcraft fear and the forms in which it could be recognized. Native Americans adopted Christian fears of diabolical witches, as it helped explain the hardships experienced in many Native communities due to disease, warfare and economic struggle. The conversion to Christian belief systems also acted as a missionary tactic to subdue Native belief systems and convert Native Americans to a more European culture.[21] However, many Native Americans adopted European beliefs in witches as an act of resistance against European colonial regimes.[22] This enabled Natives to scare European settlers in addition to explaining Indigenous plights caused by colonization as European-brought witchcraft.

The seventeenth century was a complicated period in New York State history to say the least. New York, originally called New Netherland, was not always the bustling metropolis it is today. Our state experienced many difficulties at its colonial beginnings and formed the cultural and environmental setting for events that encompassed both survival and horror. The Dutch first arrived in present-day New York around 1609, when European explorer Henry Hudson sailed his ship, the *Half Moon*, up the Hudson River, the waterway that bears his name. By 1624, the first community of Dutch foreigners from Europe had begun to form villages and establish themselves among Native Americans, calling their colony New Netherland. These Dutch settlements maintained law and order by continuing to follow the laws and ordinances of their fatherland. Dutch magistrates in the Netherlands had stopped executing people for the crime of witchcraft by the early seventeenth century. Numerous factors contributed to this new skepticism in Netherlands law and can be attributed to factors such as Erasmian philosophy and education among the secular elites, the separation of church and legal practices and the uniform legal education of the Dutch judiciary that demanded strong empirical proof for any criminal case.[23] The Dutch were skeptical of witchcraft accusations as well as the numerous accounts of violent witch trials in neighboring European countries. The early legal influence and decisions to cease witchcraft executions marked a badge of honor for Dutch heritage, and this skepticism certainly carried over with Dutch settlers beginning their colony in North America.

Shortly after Dutch arrival, settlers from New England began to populate the eastern end of Long Island. Then, in 1664, England seized control of New Netherland from the Dutch and renamed the entire colony New York, after James, Duke of York, the individual who led the charge to wrest control of the colony from the Dutch. On a larger scale, the colonies established in what we would now call the Northeast United States were under the authority of the grand empires of Europe, such as the Dutch Republic, the French and the English. The colonies were settlements created at the frontier of the unknown and continually maintained a direct relationship with the center of the empires back in Europe. In order to maintain order among the newly arriving immigrants, European colonial authorities, in essence, acted as extensions of their respective monarchs.

Some of the earliest English authorities relied greatly on religion to maintain order within the colonies. For example, Reverend John Mather codified the Law of Moses into colonial law.[24] The Law of Moses provided the earliest justification for the execution of accused witches through the verse Exodus 22:18, "Thou shalt not suffer a witch to live" (KJV). Early colonial law relied on strict interpretations of biblical verses to charge convicted criminals and help guide their sentencing. Other verses, like Leviticus 20:27, "A man also or woman that hath a familiar spirit, or that is a wizard, shall surely be put to death: they shall stone them with stones: their blood shall be upon them" (KJV), also provided theological magistrates with justification that witches existed and emphasized the importance of seeing to their execution if proven guilty. Witchcraft was a real and serious crime in seventeenth-century society, akin to the charge of murder. However, witchcraft, like homicide, was a serious and complex case to try in court and was often referred to higher courts to investigate and prosecute. The highest courts in the colonies were known as the Court of Assizes.[25] The judges of these courts were composed of the governor, the regional council, and the justices of the peace. These courts convened annually and were commissioned for Oyer and Terminer,[26] giving the judges authority to create original rulings to determine the outcome of each case. Witchcraft cases

Witchcraft: witches and devils dancing in a circle, woodcut, 1720. *Wellcome Collection.*

were often referred to this higher court to hear appeals and determine the ultimate jurisdiction in high-profile criminal matters. In 1664, Governor Richard Nicolls drafted a new code of laws for the New York colony. These laws, known as the Duke's Laws, contained the proper legal proceedings for nearly all circumstances in colonial life. However, the document was devoid of any mention of witchcraft, a likely intentional act, though for a death in which witchcraft was involved, the charge would be murder.[27]

The seventeenth century had the highest recorded frequency of accused witches in New York State history, totaling at least twenty-one individuals, with even more reports of general witchcraft suspicion. For example, during Governor Willem Kieft's tenure as director of New Netherland (1638–1647), Kieft accused the local Indigenous people of cursing him.[28] Europeans had many fears of the supernatural and associated Native American religious ceremonies and rituals to that of satanic practice. Native American healers were placed in the same categories as the malevolent witches from Europe.

Matthew Hopkins, witchfinder general, with two supposed witches calling out the names of their demons, some of which are represented by animals. Etching, 1792, after an earlier woodcut. *Wellcome Collection.*

Common characteristics of witches helped settlers identify their fears with traits and attributes that they could relate to (or assign to) accused individuals. For one, an overtly sexual theme placed witches in black masses, partaking in orgies surrounded by snakes, toads and the like. A witch was given her powers after compacting with the chief deity of evil, known as Satan in Christian religion, by signing his or her name in blood written in the deity's book. In return, the witch would be given an imp, be it undisguised or in the form of a cat, dog, ape, fox or other animal, often small and black. These imps would require constant sustenance via the witch's blood, suckled from a third teat somewhere on the witch's body. These imps were referred to as "familiars" and could wreak havoc such as aborting births, causing illness, blighting crops, raising storms, destroying structures and causing pain.[29] A witch was also given the ability to cast her spirit, similar to astral projection, and cause harm as an apparition. Witches sometimes made wax, clay or cornhusk dolls, called a poppet, in the likeness of an unknowing victim, and whatever harm caused to the poppet would be suffered by the victim, much like the popular understanding of a Voodoo doll.[30] The following accounts weave together a story of supernatural fear that gripped New York in its early settler-colonial history and set precedents for the following centuries.

2

THE JESUIT SORCERERS

Réne Goupil and Father Isaac Jogues and John de Lalande

The first Europeans to be accused of witchcraft in New York State were French Jesuit missionaries attempting to convert Native Americans to Christianity. For the Iroquois of the Mohawk Valley, the French Jesuit missionaries must have seemed so bizarre. Long-robed, bearded men muttered seemingly innocent magical incantations from a strange book in a foreign language, casting strange hand gestures over the healthy and sick alike. Anyone unfamiliar with the rituals and ceremonies of the Christian religion may understand how these missionaries were viewed as wandering sorcerers with intentions unknown—that is, until the effects of these magical gestures were realized. Days or perhaps weeks following a visit by the Jesuits, some Native Americans would fall ill due to spread of diseases often unknowingly transmitted to Indigenous communities, thus signaling a clear message that the Jesuits were in fact sorcerers and their intentions were truly malicious. Perhaps reputation preceded the Jesuit priests of the Mohawk Valley, as their fate was seemingly sealed on first contact with the Mohawk people.

The Iroquois Confederacy consists of five Indigenous nations in New York State and might better be referred to as the Haudenosaunee.[31] These Five Nations consist of the Seneca, Cayuga, Onondaga, Oneida and Mohawk; the Tuscarora joined in the early eighteenth century.[32] The French Jesuit missionaries of this account interacted primarily with Mohawk communities.

Father Isaac Jogues of Orleans, France, had heard of the hardships of the Christian proselytization efforts in New France (Canada) by Father Jean

Martyrdom of Father Isaac Jogues S.J. in Canada. Engraving by A. Millaert (Melaer) after A. van Diepenbeck (1667). *Wellcome Collection.*

de Brébeuf, who had returned to France from a recent mission to North America. Excited at the prospects of the journey through the so-called New World, Isaac Jogues was ordained and set sail for New France with several other missionaries. Jogues arrived in North America for the first time on July 2, 1636, with the sole intention of saving the "uncivilized savages" from eternal damnation. On September 11, 1636, Jogues joined Father Brébeuf's mission at the village of Saint Joseph,[33] near present-day Quebec, Canada, and fell ill with a fever shortly after arrival. This did not stop Father Jogues, and after his strength returned, he set out to save the eternal souls of the Native Americans he lived among as well as those in nearby communities. Soon after these visits, many Native Americans fell ill with smallpox, and entire villages were decimated by disease, including Saint Joseph, the village the priests had been living in. By 1637, those who had not succumbed to smallpox at Saint Joseph had abandoned the village, leaving the Jesuits to move to a new village to teach the word of Christ.[34] The Jesuits moved their operation to a new Native village called Ossossane, renamed Conception by the Jesuits. They split their time between Ossossane and another village called Teanaustayae, renamed Saint Joseph.[35] However, rumor began to spread among the Native Americans to the south that black-robed sorcerers had been exiled from Europe as harbingers of destruction and were spreading calamity through the villages they passed through. Presumably unintentionally, Jesuits likely spread diseases to many Native Americans they wished to convert to Christianity. For several more years, the Jesuits continued to tell the Native communities about the teachings of Christ.

In 1642, Father Jerome Lalemant tasked Father Jogues to accompany a convoy to Quebec to deliver letters and gather supplies for the mission. Father Jogues and the convoy of four canoes and twenty people set out on their journey for Quebec on June 2, 1642. Arriving in Quebec after losing two canoes on the journey, the party retrieved the needed supplies and picked up two lay missionaries[36] named Réne Goupil and William Couture.[37] Along the banks of the river, the convoy was ambushed by a war party of Mohawks. Jogues hid behind bushes and witnessed Réne Goupil, William Couture and several Hurons from their convoy surrender after being outnumbered. Jogues gave himself up in order to provide aid and spiritual comfort to the other prisoners. However, the Mohawks proceeded to torture Jogues in grotesque ways that surely mirrored and exceeded the horrific treatment Native prisoners had received by European captors in conflicts prior. For Jogues and Goupil, strips of flesh were cut from their thighs and arms, fingernails were pulled off, fingers were chewed on and

Statue of Isaac Jogues standing over entrance to shrine. Shrine of Our Lady of Martyrs. Auriesville, New York. *Photograph by author.*

removed with sharp shells, their skin was seared with fire and coals and they were forced to walk a gauntlet, walking between two rows of people who beat them with fists, feet and clubs as they walked by. Jogues writes how Goupil was so bloodied that only the whites of his eyes were a shade other than red.[38] The Mohawks made certain not to kill the prisoners and any injuries they sustained were treated so that further torture could ensue. The group of Mohawk prisoners, now slaves, were taken to Ossernenon, a Mohawk village along the banks of the Mohawk River (present-day Auriesville, New York). The journey to this village was arduous for the battered and stripped prisoners; their flesh peeled off from sun poisoning along the journey south to the Mohawk village.

It is important to note that Mohawk relations with the French were poor at this point in time. French regimes had allied themselves with Algonquian and Huron tribes to acquire beaver pelts used for trade with Europe. However, the Dutch had allied themselves with the Mohawks for the same

Statue of Jogues proselytizing to Mohawk children. Shrine of Our Lady of Martyrs. Auriesville, New York. *Photograph by author.*

purpose, thus further pitting the Mohawk/Dutch and Huron/Algonquian/French against each other. The beaver trade resulted in numerous battles and attacks to gain control of the market and hinder the operation of enemy efforts. French soldiers had repeatedly attacked Mohawk villages, killed many Natives and torched fields.[39] Anger and resentment of the French by the Mohawk was further galvanized by the rumors of black-robed French sorcerers sent out to spread disaster and death to every village they visited.[40] Surely, the Mohawks would have perceived the Jesuits to be a threat, as they were not only French but also sorcerers that could bewitch entire villages, threatening Mohawk society.

While at Ossernenon, Jogues and Goupil were assigned as slaves to two different families. The two mutilated Jesuits had relied heavily on their faith to get them through this arduous ordeal. In one version of the account, Goupil was unable to restrain his religious devotion and had attempted to further pursue the mission of the church at the Mohawk village, gathering the children and teaching them hand gestures, signaling the Christian sign of the cross. The grandfather of one child observed these teachings in horror and instructed his nephew to murder Goupil. On September 29, 1642, Jogues and Goupil were taking a casual walk outside of the village to discuss their faith when two Mohawks approached and told them to return to the village immediately. Realizing the tone of the Mohawk men, the Jesuits knew this might be their awaited execution and began to pray for each other on the walk back. Just before reaching the city, one of the Mohawks produced a tomahawk and swiftly cleaved[41] Réne Goupil's skull, killing him on the spot and making him the first European to be executed for witchcraft in New York.[42] Witnessing this execution, Jogues fell to his knees and awaited the same fate, but the Mohawk men told him to rise and return to the village.

As months passed, Jogues slowly gained strength as well as familiarity with the villagers; at one point, he rescued a mother and child from drowning. His religious devotion was feared as witchcraft, but he was also respected for his spiritual commitment to a practice that could get him executed. Jogues was ordered to nurse injured villagers back to health, earning him more respect in the community, to the point where he was able to slowly impart the teaching of Christ to the villagers he interacted with. A small party of Mohawks took Jogues with them on a trip to trade with the nearby Dutch fort and to fish nearby. While on this trip, Jogues received information that he was to be executed on his return to the Mohawk village. The commander of the Dutch fort had also heard this report and quickly offered Jogues a means of

Left: Execution site of Réne Goupil, plaque. Shrine of Our Lady of Martyrs. Auriesville, New York. *Photograph by author.*

Below: Execution site of Réne Goupil. Shrine of Our Lady of Martyrs. Auriesville, New York. *Photograph by author.*

escape. Jogues likely feared for his life and accepted the offer, as he may have realized his value to the French colonization efforts. After all, Jogues now had an intimate understanding of Mohawk culture, language, population estimates and military strength.[43] This information was extremely valuable to the French government. The commander instructed Jogues to return with the Mohawks and, at first chance, make for the river and board a ship whose crew would conceal him and ensure his safety. That night, the Mohawks and Jogues were offered a barn to bed down for the night. Jogues took his only possessions, which consisted of "a little office of the Blessed Virgin, an imitation of Christ, and a wooden cross" he had carved.[44] After tense conflict between the Dutch and Mohawk for capturing the Mohawk slave, Jogues, now aboard the vessel, escaped to Manhattan, where Governor Kieft welcomed him and arranged for his safe passage back to Europe.

Father Isaac Jogues did not stay in France for very long. In the spring of 1644, he returned to the missionary calling and set sail for New France once more. He was determined to convert more Native Americans to Christianity, and if he were to die doing so, he knew he would die a venerated martyr. On this trip to North America, Jogues was assigned to the village of Ville Marie (now Montreal). In July 1644, the French convened an assembly to discuss peace and included representatives from the Iroquois, Hurons, Algonquians, Montagnais and other nations. Father Jogues attended these peace talks and, after some discussion with the Iroquois ambassadors, decided to accompany them back to the Mohawk village of Ossernenon, where he had been enslaved. Although Jogues returned as a French peace envoy, he had long-term plans to convert the Mohawk people into Christians. He brought along with him a box of personal items and religious missionary vestments that he planned to leave behind at one Mohawk village along his route in order to lighten his load, intending to retrieve the items during his return visit at a later date. Father Jogues did not realize this act would lead to his own demise. In the months since he had left Ossernenon, a contagious disease wiped through the village and many surrounding villages and parasites decimated almost the entirety of the village's crops. To the Mohawk, the intentions of Father Jogues's return were clear; he was indeed a sorcerer, he wanted revenge for the torture he endured and the box he left behind was a Trojan horse that bewitched the entire village. The enraged Mohawks set out on a warpath and found Father Jogues at roughly a two-day trip away from Ossernenon. They stripped him and tortured him and his companions, which included lay missionary John de Lalande, and decided his fate over the following days. On October 18, 1646, Jogues was instructed to enter a cabin; as the priest crossed the threshold, a Mohawk man struck him from behind with a tomahawk to his skull. Jogues died immediately. The following day, John de Lalande met the same fate.

Interestingly enough, the site of the first of New York's accused witches (or sorcerers) and consequential Jesuit martyrdom, is now a holy shine located in Auriesville, New York. The shrine compound is known today as Our Lady of Martyrs Shine and is frequented by Christian pilgrims during a scheduled pilgrimage season between April and October. The area contains a collection of buildings dedicated to the holy prayer and remembrance of the Christian-focused historical narratives that transpired in this one-time Mohawk village. The area includes the hill where the Jesuit priests were beaten, two separate "Stations of the Cross" areas (one of which leads up to the execution site of Réne Goupil), a chapel, a coliseum shrine containing within the black box of Father Jogues that condemned him and of course a gift shop where one can buy T-shirts inscribed with the names of the Jesuit priests executed at this site.

3

THE LONG ISLAND SACHEMS

Sachem Poggatacut and Wyandanch's Agent

Any casual internet search of witchcraft on Long Island, New York, may produce one or two accounts of witchcraft. However, on Long Island alone, there have been nine recorded accounts of witchcraft accusations (or at least suspicions). While some, as we will examine later, are merely fictional stories invented over the years, many are rooted in actual historical events. The first account of witchcraft accusation on Long Island happened in 1650 and involved Mohegan sachem[45] Uncas accusing Poggatacut, "the Mohansick Sachem of Long Island," of bewitching him.[46] Later, the Niantic sachem, Ninigret, stated that Poggatacut's younger brother, and later grand sachem, Wyandanch, had hired a witch to assassinate Uncas. The reference to the leader of the Mohansick appears only once in the historical record and likely refers to the Manhasset people (present-day Shelter Island, New York), the leader of which was Sachem Poggatacut.[47] The life of Poggatacut was complex, as he operated in a highly stressful and rapidly changing environment that included European colonization, tribal adaptation and warfare. Native Americans have highly adaptable communities that resisted colonial expansion pressures and played off European fears and anxieties to disrupt European regimes, maintain their ways of life and conqueror enemy tribes. The severity of European witchcraft paranoia in the seventeenth century was no secret to the Native Americans, and Sachem Poggatacut soon found himself among the accused.

Poggatacut was born sometime around 1568, and by the 1640s, he had become a grand sachem on Eastern Long Island, uniting four Long Island

Grave of Lion Gardiner. South End Burying Ground. East Hampton, New York. *Photograph by author.*

tribes and acting as the signatory for European settler land deeds. It was in fact Poggatacut and his wife, Aswaw, who deeded land to Lion Gardiner in 1639, what would later be known as Gardiner's Island (see the later the account of Elizabeth Garlick),[48] and Poggatacut was later the lead signatory of Shelter Island.[49] He signed his name "Sachem of Paumonoc," Paumonoc being the Indigenous name for Long Island, though he also went by the names "Yokee" or "Youghco" and lived on Sachem's Neck on Shelter Island.[50]

During this period, Native Americans on Long Island were masters and shapers of their environment. They were (and continue to be) experts at hunting, fishing and foraging and supplemented these primary methods of subsistence with farming and landscape management.[51] Their healthcare came from a knowledge of home remedies and the abundant natural pharmacopeia accessible to them throughout the landscape, combined with spiritual prayer. The social structure before European arrival was likely composed of many extended family groups that were all interconnected through a web of exogamous marriages that spanned all of Long Island, southern Connecticut and southern Rhode Island.[52] Some of these families would join together for only brief moments to participate in large hunting or war parties. It wasn't until European arrival on Long Island that clearly defined tribes were invented and encouraged by European regimes in order to create a directed strategy for acquiring land from Native Americans,[53] thus displacing their communities; this was just one approach of many in the early forms of settler colonialism, the legacies of which still persist in the Americas today.

Samson Occum, a Christian Native American minister and missionary, wrote "An Account of Montauk Indians" in the 1760s,[54] in which he discussed the culture of Montauk Indians and made comparisons between Christianity and Native American religion. Occum writes, "There was a god over their corn, another over the beans, another over their pumpkins, and squashes, etc. There was a god over their wigwams, another of the wind, one of the fire, another over the sea, one of the day, and another of the night." Further, Occum states that there was a belief in a supreme god that ruled over the others called Cauhluntoowut and also an "evil" god of mischief called Mutcheshesunnetooh.[55] Spiritual ceremonies occurred once or twice a year in early June when the corn was close to being ripe.[56] These ceremonies, called *powaws* were overseen by religious leaders with the same name. Occum describes extraordinary feats of daring during these events, such as the powaws inducing hypnosis in Indigenous men whereby they were impervious to injury:

> *Sometimes they would run into the water; sometimes into the fire; and at other times, run to the top of high trees and tumble-down head-long to the ground, yet receive no hurt by all these. And I don't see for my part, why it is not as true, as the English or other nation's witchcraft, but is a great mystery of darkness.*[57]

Native Americans employed a wide range of native plants for medicinal purposes. For example, a tea made from spruce branch tips was high in vitamin C and cured scurvy during the winter months, and sassafras was used for treating venereal diseases. Ginseng was another common herb that was a familiar medicinal plant for the Europeans, and its discovery in the Americas proved to be financially beneficial for early settlers and merchants.[58]

European jurisdiction in this region was divided into several colonies, such as Connecticut Colony/River Colony, New Haven Colony, Massachusetts Bay Colony, Plymouth Colony and New Netherland (later New York). These European colonies would often convene as a federation to discuss mutual issues, calling themselves the United Colonies of New England (excluding Dutch-controlled New Netherland). However, the seventeenth century was a highly complex period in the northeastern United States and cannot be reduced to simple Algonquian versus English interests[59] without invoking a European-biased perspective of history. Algonquian tribes of this region were numerous, including Mohegan, Narragansett, Niantic, Montaukett, Shinnecock, Pequot and others. Algonquian leaders frequently employed new strategies of wresting control over their tribal enemies by weaving themselves into the constant feuding that occurred between the various and disparate European colonial authorities.[60] Native American tribes were pressured to align themselves with European regimes in response to the lethal and savage demonstration of European military organization and technology during the Pequot War of 1637, in which the Pequot people were nearly decimated.[61] For the Native Americans, these alliances ensured European protection from enemy tribes and colonial forces while also allowing access to better trading opportunities with European allies. For the Europeans, these alliances facilitated compliance with land transfers and European sovereignty over Indigenous land and military allies against attacking tribal enemies. Sachem Poggatacut and his brother Sachem Wyandanch, for example, formed an alliance with an English mercenary and fort builder named Lion Gardiner who had first visited Montaukett territory in 1639. Through his land dealings and exploits, Gardiner became the most prominent landowner and leader in the region. This alliance helped Wyandanch eventually gain control over his tribal neighbors on Long Island and become recognized as the sachem of all Long Island tribes. Meanwhile, other New England tribes formed alliances with their colonial neighbors as well. Sachem Uncas of the Mohegans formed an alliance with the English in Connecticut Colony, Sachem Miantonomi of the Narragansett formed an alliance with Massachusetts Bay Colony and Sachem Ninigret of the Niantic allied his tribe with Roger Williams's colony in Rhode Island.

Sachem Uncas frequently appeared at the sessions of the United Colonies of New England to register complaints against his rivals, and in 1650, he reported that his enemies had bewitched him and his men and the "Mohansick" sachem of Long Island (Poggatacut), was behind it.[62] The transcript reads as follows:

> *Uncus Sachem of the Mohegins Informed the Commissioners and complained that the Mohanasick Sachem in Long Island had killed [the] son of the said Uncus, his men, bewitched divers others and himself also and desired the Commissions that he might be Righted therein. But because*

Map of Connecticut and the New England Colonies in the 1640s. *From the book* Voices from Colonial America: Connecticut, 1614–1776, *published by National Geographic Society 2007, National Geographic Books.*

the said Sachem of Long Island was not present to answer for himself it was thought meet and accordingly advised that Commission be granted by the Government of Connecticut to Captain John Mason, Mr. Howell, Mr. Gosmer and Thomas Benedict of Southhold or any three of them to examine the matters Charged by Uncus and if prove be Clear to labor to Convince them thereof Require satisfaction and in Case of reasonable Compliance to endeavor a Composure thereof; but if no satisfaction will be given for Injuries proved then to let them to know they give the English Just Cause of offence and will bring trouble upon themselves.
—*September 1650*[63]

Poggatacut and Uncas had a contentious relationship dating back to before the Pequot War in 1636, when Poggatacut sent Uncas sixty fathoms of wampum[64] to present to Governor Winthrop, with twenty fathoms for Uncas to keep as payment. Uncas decided to keep it all, thereby angering Poggatacut and prompting a colonial investigation.[65] The 1650 witchcraft accusation of Poggatacut was short-lived, as colonial authorities had little interest in tribal disputes. Poggatacut's health was already declining, and he passed away sometime around 1653, thus contributing to his younger brother Wyandanch's increase in political power around the same time. Uncas and the other New England sachems soon diverted more attention to Wyandanch and attempted to use similar strategies to destabilize Wyandanch's authority on Long Island. Wyandanch was a clever leader and negotiator in his own right. Through European political allies like Lion Gardiner, he was able to obtain leadership over the Indigenous communities of Long Island and soon became a formidable enemy to the New England sachems. Wyandanch resisted physical and political threats and attacks to his authority while navigating the entangled politics of the European colonial governments as well as the Niantic and Mohegan tribes. In 1656, Sachem Ninigret sent his agent Newcom to the colonial courts to file several complaints against Wyandanch. These claims included accusing Wyandanch of an unsolved murder of an Englishman named Drake, breaking a tribal peace treaty and hiring a witch to kill Sachem Uncas.[66] Wyandanch was summoned to the United Colonies' court to answer for these allegations, but neither Ninigret nor Uncas appeared to testify against him. Further, the witnesses named in the witchcraft charge recanted their story and some never appeared in court. One witness claimed an individual named Wampeague confessed to being hired by Wyandanch to kill the Englishman Drake, but Wampeague never appeared at court, leading to all charges against Wyandanch being dropped.[67] Wyandanch lived out the rest of his life on Long Island.

Poggatacut's death in 1653 prompted a ceremonial funeral in his honor, and his body was carried from Shelter Island to be buried in Montauk. Along the way, the Native pallbearers stopped along a footpath for the night and marked the spot where the grand sachem's body had lain by digging a hole twelve inches deep, eighteen inches wide.[68] This spot soon became hallowed ground and was venerated by the Indigenous community, as noted by European observer Daniel Denton in 1670 and later accounts into the mid-nineteenth century.[69] That is, it was until 1860, when a turnpike was constructed and the site demolished. What was once regarded as Sachems Hole was destroyed, and a historic place placard was erected close to the

Council Rock at Fort Hill Cemetery. Montauk, New York. *Photograph by author.*

spot on along the road in 1935. The inaccurate and misspelled text claimed the spot as Whopping Boy Hollow and placed Poggatacut's death in 1651.[70] The historical marker can be seen at 40° 58.912' N, 72° 15.057' W, along the east side of East Hampton Sag Harbor Turnpike, Route 114. Sachem Wyandanch is likely buried at the Montaukett ancestral burial grounds at the Fort Hill Cemetery in Montauk. This area was once the meeting place for sachems, and a monument stands within the cemetery acknowledging the spot's Indigenous significance.

Today, the east end of Long Island is characterized by multimillion-dollar homes, world-renowned golf courses and coastlines that serve as a backdrop for some of the most impressive yachts in the world. The town centers are picturesque areas of commerce with expensive restaurants, name-brand designer stores, cozy cafés and art galleries underscoring the local sense of privilege, elitism and exclusivity. In contemporary American culture, a home in the Hamptons is a symbol of status and prestige. While the ultrarich enjoy the unrestricted mobility of the Hamptons, the Indigenous communities who live there today are confined to a lowland reservation nestled in a small corner of the region, threatened by rising sea levels, all the while their sacred lands and ancestral burials are constantly desecrated by increasing real estate development, threatening Long Island Indigenous culture and sovereignty. Marginalization and discrimination have been occurring over the last four hundred years, as demonstrated within the stories of the historical individuals mentioned in this chapter.

4

CORNELIS MELYN (MOOLYN)

Cornelis Melyn was a respectable patroon (similar to a landlord) and early settler of Staten Island, New York. Cornelis hailed from Antwerp, Belgium (then part of the Spanish Netherlands), and was born on September 17, 1600. By age twenty-seven, he was an established tailor and soon married Janneken Adriaens,[71] with whom he had several children. Cornelis's first journey to New Netherland failed when his ship was captured by pirates and thus forced to return to the Netherlands. On his second attempt, he successfully arrived in New Netherland with his family and, with forty-one other people, established the new colony of Staten Island.

For a brief period during the Dutch occupation of New York (formerly known as New Netherland), Director (similar to a governor) Willem Kieft (1638–1647) ruled with particularly jingoistic policies, waging war on Native American communities he deemed problematic. In fact, it was Director Kieft who deeded all of Staten Island to Cornelis Melyn.[72] However, Kieft's horrendous reign was protested by the settlers whose lives were upended due to his political decisions. Historian Russell Shorto states, "He [Kieft] was not a politician. He arrived with a directive to turnaround a failing corporate venture, and he arrived with one arrow in his quiver."[73] In an effort to appease the settlers of New Netherland, Kieft appointed a council of eight of the most respectable men in the colony, including Cornelis Melyn, to help generate public support. This

Mural in Staten Island Borough Hall depicting Cornelis Melyn trading with Native Americans. Staten Island, New York. *Photograph of mural courtesy of the Office of Staten Island Borough president Vito J. Fossella, Department of Press and Communications.*

council was predominately for appearances, as he did not heed the advice of this council when making political decisions. During this period, Kieft's decisions and approach to Native relations resulted in what was later termed Kieft's War, which resulted in the merciless slaughter of Native Americans by European forces and the resulting attacks on European settlements by retaliating Native Americans.[74] Lenape warriors destroyed the Staten Island settlement, forcing settlers to flee. Cornelis Melyn and his family temporarily relocated to Manhattan along the East River near the intersection of Broad and Pearl Streets. Kieft was ultimately recalled to Amsterdam to answer for his crimes, but en route, his ship sank, and he was lost to the sea. Kieft was replaced with Peter Stuyvesant, who was left to clean up Kieft's political mess, including the poor European-Native relations and land disputes within the colony. Unfortunately for Melyn, his involvement with Kieft, however contentious it was, made the incoming governor uneasy when dealing with him. In following years, Stuyvesant banished Cornelis Melyn for the crime of *lèse-majesté* (offense against the majesty) and sent him back to Europe. The ship ran aground off the coast of Wales, though Melyn survived and was able to fight his conviction and return to the Staten Island colony.

Melyn returned with his same goal: to build up the colony of Staten Island. Tensions with the Lenape people were still hostile, and he only made matters worse by spreading rumors among the Native Americans of hostile European intentions.[75]

> *In 1652, Reverend Wilhelmus Grasmeer would comment that he "had heard the Manhattans Indians of New Netherland, living at Nayak, a place on Long Island directly opposite Staten Island, frequently say that the said Cornelis Melyn had made them believe and declared to them, Director Petrus Stuyvesant would, as soon as he had built a wall around Fort Amsterdam, come to kill them, namely the savages, whereupon the said savages fled and came armed to Gravesend."*[76]

In 1653, the Lenape once again attacked the Staten Island settlements. They were convinced Melyn was a sorcerer who was poisoning their people and sold them defective guns and gunpowder. The Lenape attacked Dutch settlers and were prepared to eradicate the source (Cornelis Melyn) and the rest of the European settlers on Staten Island to prevent further bewitchment at the hands of the Christians.[77]

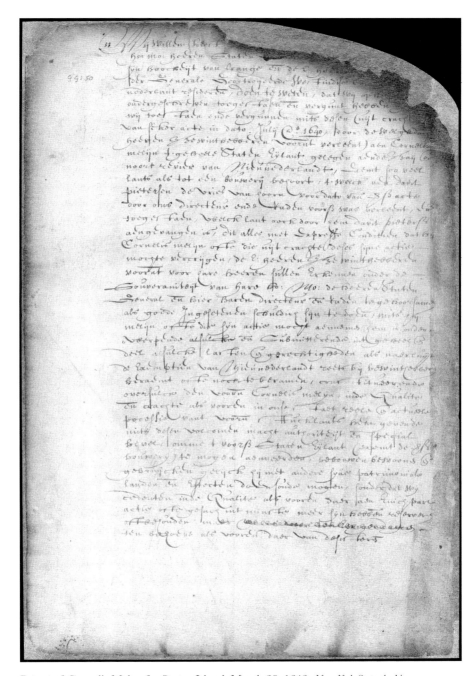

Patent of Cornelis Melyn for Staten Island, March 28, 1642. *New York State Archives.*

Stuyvesant's writings state:

> *But the absolute assertion and allegation of the remonstrates that murders had been committed by the Indians, under the pretense of not having been paid for their land, is made entirely without foundation and in bad faith. If the remonstrates were inclined to tell the truth or to investigate, they would find that the three murders recently committed on Staten Island by the Indians were perpetrated because the Indians claim that Moolyn [Cornelis Melyn[78]] is a sorcerer, that he has poisoned them, that he has sold bad powder and guns and so forth; consequently, the Indians from the south have all sworn to kill him and all the people on Staten Island.[79]*

Staten Island settlements were once again destroyed during the Peach Tree War in 1655, and Melyn, frustrated, admitted defeat and moved his family to New Haven, Connecticut Colony, and swore allegiance to England.[80] There he lived out the rest of his days with his family. Cornelis Melyn's son, Jacob, has a particularly interesting history as well, getting in trouble twice for his lothario ways. First, he was charged for "flirting outrageously" with a woman named Sarah Tuttle and later reprimanded for seducing Hannah Hubbard of Wethersfield (his future wife) with "a cunny and intentional misreading of Scripture."[81]

5

GOODWIFE ELIZABETH GARLICK

lizabeth Garlick of Southampton, Long Island, is perhaps the most notorious "witch" in New York history. Her bestowed title *Goody* is the shortened form of *Goodwife*, which was a polite form of address for a woman of middle- or lower-class status during the seventeenth century. The masculine form is *Goodman*. And for a woman of a higher social rank, the polite form would be *Mistress*. Elizabeth Garlick is known by history and folklore as Goody Garlick. Her maiden name was likely Blanchard.[82] The child of French Huguenots escaping persecution, Elizabeth would have already been viewed as different or an outsider due to her ancestry by the predominantly English Puritans of New England.[83] Surviving records from the early seventeenth century are rare, and Elizabeth's age at the time of her witchcraft accusation (1658) is difficult to estimate. However, it is believed by some scholars that she was no younger than forty-five and no older than fifty-five during this examined period of her life.[84] Her older age would have also made her an outsider, considering over half the population of East Hampton was under twenty-five in 1657.[85]

Many settlers of early East Hampton had arrived together from an older settlement in Lynn, Massachusetts. Close relationships were common in this group along with the accompanying petty disputes and old gossip. According to one settler, Goody Simons, suspicion of Elizabeth Garlick started back when they were living in Lynn. Goody Simons had some unspecified medical issue that caused her to experience seizures, and when she was given medicinal herbs to remedy her condition, she saw a "black thing" enter her house. A neighbor exclaimed, "Who owns a black cat?" and someone replied, "Goody Garlick."[86] These women believed that the black form was Elizabeth Garlick's black cat and quite possible a witch's familiar.[87] This encounter surely aroused suspicions, but shortly after this event, the settlers began the journey to East Hampton to form a new village, thus temporarily pausing any suspicions and the idle time often needed in the growth of town gossip. However, once in East Hampton, Goody Simons did not forget, and the next time she had seizures, her superstitious zeal prevented her from accepting any herbal remedies.

In East Hampton, neighbor Goody Bishop heard that Goody Simons was having a seizure, ran to Elizabeth Garlick's home to receive some dock weed (a medicinal herb) and promptly ran over to the Simons house to deliver the potential remedy. Goody Bishop arrived at the Simons house but was not welcomed with relief by Goody Simons. Instead, Simons was repulsed by the herbs and threw them into the fire with the support of an accompanying friend, Goody Davis. Simons then claimed that she wanted nothing to do with Elizabeth Garlick anymore. In this situation, the herb on trial was dock weed (*Rumex* spp. L.), though it is certainly possible that the historical record may have mistaken this for duckweed (*Spirodela polyrhiza* L.), both of which had recorded medicinal uses during this period.[88] Dock weed was used for "cleansing the blood and liver" and as a remedy for "those that spit blood,"[89] while duckweed was thought to decrease harmful or uncomfortable fluids (known then as humors) in the body.[90] Today, it is also known that duckweed has fever-lowering effects and can also be used to treat body aches.[91] It is also known that dock weed can be used as a blood purifier, for whooping cough, contraceptive and a laxative.[92] These plants are also prescribed for similar symptoms by the Iroquois people.[93] Regardless of which plant was prescribed to Goody Simons, the adverse effects, combined with a fear of the supernatural, may have persuaded Simons that Garlick meant her more harm than help.

Goody Davis was perhaps the most suspicious of Elizabeth Garlick's actions. Davis had been widowed twice and had recently lost a child due to some unspecified sickness. Infant mortality was at an all-time high during this period, and losing a child was unfortunately all too common. Nevertheless, mothers were naturally and justifiably protective and anxious about the health of their infants. Goody Davis was a young first-time mother when Elizabeth commented on her infant's beauty, then remarked that the sounds the infant made were concerning and that Davis's child might be ill. Goody Davis was shaken by this observation and interpreted Garlick's

Witchcraft: the devil bringing medicine to a man or woman in bed. Woodcut, 1720. *Wellcome Collection.*

remark as a bewitchment; the suspicion was further enflamed when the baby died five days later. Elizabeth Garlick's remark was (presumably) out of concern, though Davis attributed it to the "evil eye," a death warning and hex performed out of jealousy and envy—in this case, of the infant's beauty.[94] From then on, a grieving Goody Davis began to see bewitchment in everything relating to Elizabeth Garlick.

Sometime later, Elizabeth and her husband, Joshua Garlick, moved to Gardiner's Island, where they worked for Lion Gardiner, though this move was not without its own issues. Lion Gardiner sued the Garlick family for "slanderous speech," though this matter was peaceable resolved. However, shortly after this lawsuit, Goody Davis began to attribute a series of strange events to an allegedly spiteful Elizabeth Garlick. For example, Lion Gardiner's ox broke its leg, an enslaved African child went missing, a pig died during childbirth and a man died due to unknown causes, but to the suspicion of Goody Davis, Elizabeth Garlick's witchcraft was the cause of it all.[95] Interestingly, Davis and her friends performed a kind of "counter-magic" to discover the identity of the witch or rather to confirm Garlick's guilt.[96] They performed a ritual by burning the tail hair of the deceased mother pig (a suspected victim of Garlick's bewitchment), which theoretically would cause pain to the witch herself and prompt her to show up to the ritual to investigate the origin of the counter-bewitchment and her resultant pain. In this small village, after an unknown period of waiting, Elizabeth Garlick eventually passed by the home where the ritual was conducted, thereby confirming their suspicion. It is also unclear how the town women viewed this counter-magic ritual as religiously acceptable in such a contentiously pious period of history.

Whispers and rumor radiated through the village. Was Garlick truly a witch? No one—except Goody Davis, who was certain—was sure. Soon the hard work and thriftiness of the Garlick family afforded them property within the village. Originally being of lower status, the Garlicks had lived farther away from the town square, but with time and money they were able to afford property closer to the town center. The most affluent citizens of East Hampton village lived closest to the church, just north of Hook Pond near the current Town Pond, while lower-class individuals lived farther away.[97] To illustrate this, the provided town map shows the affluent Gardiner family located near the center of the map nearest the church, while the Garlick family is found more north, farther from the church but still within the vicinity. The perceived "success," demonstrated by the Garlicks moving closer into town and not terribly far from the church, was once more seen as another supernatural act of personal gain. Further, Garlick was suspected of infanticide with the death of any baby that occurred within the town. Goody Davis excited the situation further by telling the mothers of the deceased that their previous interactions with Garlick may be the root cause of their children's misfortune.

In February 1657, Samuel Parsons stopped by the Howell household to visit Arthur Howell. However, Arthur was not home, and his wife, Elizabeth Howell, née Gardiner, invited Samuel to wait by the hearth fire until her husband returned home. She informed Samuel that she was suffering from a headache and might be getting a bit sick. Samuel left to allow Elizabeth to rest and decided to return later to see if Arthur had returned home. However, Elizabeth's condition worsened, and when Arthur arrived back at the house, he found her wrapped in blankets and lying near the fire. Arthur and his friend William Russel carried Elizabeth to her bed.

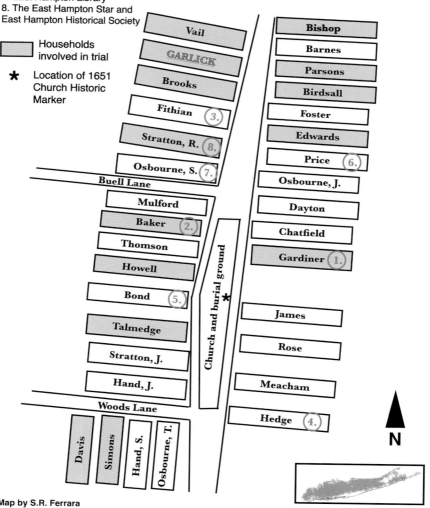

Current Notable Buisnesses and Landmarks
1. Lion Gardiner Mill Cottage
2. The Baker House 1650
3. 1770 House Restaurant & Inn
4. The Hedges Inn
5. The Maidstone
6. Guild Hall
7. East Hampton Library
8. The East Hampton Star and East Hampton Historical Society

Households involved in trial

★ Location of 1651 Church Historic Marker

Map of home-lots in East Hampton, Long Island, ca. 1658
showing the accused witch, Goodwife Elizabeth Garlick, and trial participants

Vail · Bishop
GARLICK · Barnes
Brooks · Parsons
Fithian (3.) · Birdsall
Stratton, R. (8.) · Foster
Osbourne, S. (7.) · Edwards
Buell Lane · Price (6.)
Mulford · Osbourne, J.
Baker (2.) · Dayton
Thomson · Chatfield
Howell · Gardiner (1.)
Bond (5.)
Talmedge · James
Stratton, J. · Rose
Hand, J. · Meacham
Woods Lane · Hedge (4.)
Davis · Simons · Hand, S. · Osbourne, T.

Church and burial ground ★

N

Map by S.R. Ferrara
Based on Osbourne's map in Town Records of East Hampton Vol.II (1887) **Map not to scale
and Demos' *Entertaining Satan* (2004)

Map of home lots in East Hampton, Long Island, circa 1658, showing the accused witch, Goodwife Elizabeth Garlick, and trial participants. *Courtesy of author, based on J. Demos map (2004).*

Witchcraft: witches giving babies to the devil. Woodcut, 1720. *Wellcome Collection.*

Elizabeth Howell was the sixteen-year-old daughter of the famed Lion Gardiner, the most prominent person in East Hampton and perhaps the region at the time. She had married Arthur Howell and recently given birth to their first child. Elizabeth's fever combined with stress might have sparked a hallucination, and the already-circulating rumors of Goody Garlick may have inspired Elizabeth to direct blame toward Garlick for her torment.

Elizabeth Howell was lying in bed, surrounded by friends, and singing psalms to ease her suffering, when suddenly she cried out, "A witch! A witch! Now you are come to torture me because I spoke two or three words against you! In the morning you will come fawning." Her husband's friend Samuel Parsons quickly replied, "The Lord be merciful to her….It is well if she be not bewitched." Lion Gardiner was alerted of the issue and visited to comfort his daughter. While bedside, Lion noticed his daughter fearfully staring at the foot of her bed before screaming once more, "A witch! A witch!" and exclaiming that a "black thing" was near the foot of her bed. She attempted to ambush the unseen creature but was held back by her husband. While Elizabeth's condition worsened, Lion told his wife, Mary Gardiner, of the situation; she also happened to be very sick. Mary used what little strength she had to walk to her daughter's house and comfort her. Elizabeth told her mother, "Oh Mother, I am bewitched," to which Mary replied, "No, no, you are [just] asleep or dreaming." Elizabeth insisted that she was in fact bewitched, and her mother asked her to then name who she saw. After some deliberation, Elizabeth replied, "Goody Garlick! Goody Garlick! I can see her at the far corner of the bed, and a black thing of hers at the other corner." Mary replied, "Hush child, this is a terrible thing you say."

Mary's own condition was still poor, and she returned home. However, on the same day shortly after Mary left, three neighbors stopped by to check on Elizabeth's condition: Goody Birdsall, Ann Edwards and Goody Simons. Young Elizabeth told them exactly what they wanted to hear. She cried out, "She is a double-tongued woman….She pricks me with pins….Oh! She torments me!" The three women asked Elizabeth who was torturing her. After some dramatic reluctancy, Elizabeth wailed, "Ah, Garlick, you jeered me when I came to your house to call my husband home. You laughed and jeered me, and I went crying away." Elizabeth continued, "Oh, you are a pretty one…. Send for Garlick and his wife! I would tear her to pieces and leave the birds to pick her bones." The women encouraged her fever-induced delirium and asked why she would do such a thing to Goody Garlick. Elizabeth replied, "Did you not see here last night by my bedside, ready to pull me to pieces? She pricked me with pins, and she brought a black thing to the foot of my bed." Elizabeth then began to choke, and Ann Edwards quickly attempted to force open her mouth with the handle of a knife. After successfully prying Elizabeth's mouth open, Edwards administered a sugar and oil solution thought to remedy the effects of bewitchment.[98] Elizabeth then coughed, and the women saw a pin produced from her mouth. However, this mysterious pin is surrounded by some controversy. Goody Simons was the individual to retrieve the pin from Elizabeth's mouth, but only Goody Birdsall and Ann Edwards testified to this event. It is likely that Goody Simons used sleight of hand to produce the pin in an attempt to reap payback for the past aggression by Elizabeth Garlick.[99] The fact that at later testimonies, Simons *did not* testify to the pin event may indicate some guilt in orchestrating a lie.

Goody Birdsall and Ann Edwards returned home after the dramatic events of Elizabeth Howell naming Garlick as her tormentor and coughing out a pin. However, Goody Simons stayed with Howell that night to comfort her in her last hours. Elizabeth's husband, Arthur Howell, along with his friend

William Russell and their enslaved servant Boose, stood watch over her that night. Throughout the night, they were spooked by two incidents neither Elizabeth Howell nor Goody Simons were awake for. The first incident sounded like wood scratching coming from under Elizabeth's bed with no justifiable cause. The second incident sounded like rumbling coming from within the fireplace. Arthur described it "[as if] a great rock were thrown down on a heap of stones, but found no place to rest."

Elizabeth's condition worsened, and as she lay dying, she muttered, "Garlick…double-tongued…ugly thing…pins," until she eventually succumbed to her illness. Once Elizabeth Howell was laid to rest, the local magistrates convened at the meetinghouse to address the claim that Elizabeth Garlick murdered Elizabeth Howell with witchcraft. The townsfolk testified to the events that prompted the accusation. However, there is no record of Lion Gardiner testifying. Nor is there any testimony from Goody Davis, who was the chief accuser and gossip spreader. In fact, Goody Davis seems to have made peace with Elizabeth Garlick, stating in her testimony, "[She has] brought many things to me….and she is very kind to me," and after all, "She were as good to please the Devil as anger him,"[100] which could be interpreted as a spiteful way of saying, "It's probably best to please my enemy instead of upsetting her." This was likely a wise strategy for Goody

Site of First Church and Meeting House, where Goody Garlicks first examination would have taken place. South End Burying Ground. East Hampton, New York. *Photograph by author.*

Davis, as she was now facing charges for slander brought against her by Elizabeth's husband, Joshua Garlick, and supported by several other men in the village. Furthermore, Lion Gardiner commented that Goody Davis might be responsible for the death of her own child by selling her breast milk for wampum.[101] Even so, Goody Garlick was not out of danger quite yet. There was still some suspicion surrounding Elizabeth Garlick's involvement in the death, and the magistrates of East Hampton were inexperienced with this sort of criminal charge involving spectral evidence. Therefore, they deferred the case to the higher court in Connecticut, and Goody Garlick was escorted there by Lion Gardiner as well as John Hand and Thomas Baker, three of the most reputable members of East Hampton.[102] In Connecticut, the indictment read as follows:

> *Elizabeth Garlick, thou art indicted by the name of Elizabeth Garlick the wife of Joshua Garlick of East Hampton, that not having the fear of God before thine eyes thou hast entertained familiarity with Satan, the Great enemy of God and mankind, and by his help since the year 1650 hath done works above the course of nature to the loss of lives of several persons (with several other sorceries), and in particular the wife of Arthur Howell of East Hampton, for which, according to the laws of God and the established law of this Commonwealth, thou deservest to die.*[103]

Elizabeth Garlick likely feared for her life, as the Connecticut court had a reputation for executing accused witches.[104] It can only be speculated that she worried about what her fate would be during the short period of time she was incarcerated before the trial. The case was heard likely on May 5, 1658, by seven magistrates and a jury of twelve men.[105] Luckily, one of the magistrates was John Winthrop Jr., who was participating in a witchcraft trial for the first time. John Winthrop Jr. was not only a magistrate but also a reputable scientist, alchemist, philosopher and physician who treated the poor for free.[106] Interestingly, John Winthrop Jr. was not a stranger to the defendant or even to Lion Gardiner. In fact, it was Winthrop who had invited Lion Gardiner to leave England and move to Connecticut to build the fort at Saybrook.[107] Both men continued a profitable relationship, as Lion Gardiner sent Winthrop livestock, wampum and other valuable goods. What's even more interesting is that the intermediary who facilitated the exchange and payment was none other than Joshua Garlick, Elizabeth's husband.[108] However, there is no record of John Winthrop Jr.'s opinion of the Garlick family. Nevertheless, it is safe to say that Elizabeth Garlick was

John Winthrop. *The New York Public Library Digital Collections.*

already a familiar name when Winthrop was first brought on to try the case. Elizabeth's good fortune did not end there, as it appears that the court environment possessed all the right conditions for an acquittal, likely by happenstance and not by design. We do not know for sure if any of the women or accusers of East Hampton attended the trials in Connecticut, but we do know that the town's most respected men were there, as they had escorted Elizabeth Garlick to the court, although they made the journey with political motives, to establish a relationship between East Hampton and Connecticut. Their appearance at her trial certainly humanized her in the face of the jury and judges.[109]

Ultimately, Elizabeth Garlick was not convicted of witchcraft and certainly not executed for it. However, she was not acquitted of the charges either. It was ordered that her husband, Joshua, should pay a large bond to assure the court of his wife's good behavior and that she should appear in court, either Connecticut or East Hampton, for periodic appearances to ensure she was upholding this agreement. John Winthrop Jr. commented, "The Christian care and prudence of those in authority with you in search into ye case according to such just suspicions as appeared."[110]

The Puritan magistrates and jury were unable to make a connection between Elizabeth Garlick and Satan. The accusations made against her by the women of East Hampton referenced only events of "harmful magic" and made no reference to Garlick signing her name in the book of the devil or meeting with other witches on the Sabbath.[111] The Puritan orthodoxy did not subscribe to the idea that a farmer's wife could conjure up such supernatural power by her own means, and since the devil was not explicitly named, she was cleared. The Connecticut court even went so far as to instruct the settlers of East Hampton to mend their relationship with the Garlick family, commenting:

> *We think good to certify that it is desired and expected by this court that you should carry neighborly and peaceably without just offence to [Joshua] Garlick and his wife and that they should do the like to you.*[112]

Goody Elizabeth Garlick returned to East Hampton with a newfound power. The women who had accused and persecuted her now realized the court would not be able to help them rid Garlick from their lives. The courts did not acquit her case but instead vindicated her actions and in so many words ordered that the entire village should be nicer to Joshua and Elizabeth Garlick, thus making Elizabeth Garlick appear invincible.[113] Garlick's accusers were defeated, and they ultimately decided to make peace with the Garlick family. New England history has shown that accused witches and their families often suffered from financial and social hardship after their trials and moved to new villages to escape gossip and slander. However, the Garlick family experienced quite the opposite, as they thrived in East Hampton following Elizabeth's return.[114] Joshua went back to work as an intermediary between Winthrop and Gardiner while also expanding his land holdings and financial assets. Joshua and Elizabeth Garlick lived in East Hampton until their deaths around the year 1700; both lived to nearly one hundred years old.[115] Their home, according to the town map, was likely somewhere in the vicinity of 135 or 127 Main Street (west side of the road), East Hampton, New York. Today there sits a multimillion-dollar home in one of the most affluent neighborhoods in the entire United States.

South End Burying Ground. East Hampton, New York. *Photograph by author.*

Elizabeth and Joshua Garlick's resting place is unknown but likely would have been South End Burying Ground. However, there are no identifiable grave markers that indicate a resting place for the Garlicks. The study of graves or tombstones has much to offer in valuable historical and anthropological data, but the absence of a grave marker, particularly in a location you would expect to find one, may also offer just as much valuable information. This examination of the invisible underscores, presumably, the sentiments of not only those who laid Elizabeth to rest but also how we as a community choose to remember (or forget) more painful or embarrassing memories. This absence of an identifiable resting place may be due to natural causes like erosion or perhaps was a deliberate attempt to silence a particular heritage of East Hampton community actions and anxieties.

6

MARY WRIGHT ANDREWS

It may be a little misleading to place Mary Wright Andrews's name in this book. After all, it is likely she was not accused of witchcraft at all. In fact, if the pages of history are so determined to immortalize her, then it should be for her bravery while battling a government that denied her rights as a woman and a Quaker. So why investigate her as a witch? Well, in 1843, historian Benjamin Thompson attributed witchcraft accusations to Mary Wright Andrews of Oyster Bay. It is not certain what led Thompson to this conclusion, and perhaps we may never know, as he did not provide any footnotes or sources for his claim. This connection has since been used by witchcraft historians to add Mary to lists of accused witches but also criticize the authenticity of the supposed witchcraft accusation in the historical record.[116] Thompson offers only one paragraph to describe Mary's witchcraft history, which reads as follows:

> But in the year 1660, suspicions fell upon one Mary Wright, a poor and ignorant woman of Oyster Bay, and it became a matter of very grave consideration, that a crime so enormous should undergo a rigid investigation. There being no tribunal in this quarter competent, in the opinion of the people, to hear, try, and determine a business of such magnitude, it was resolved to transport the accused to the general court of Massachusetts, where charges of this sort were supposed to be better understood. She was arraigned there soon after, and although the evidence of the guilt of witchcraft failed, she was convicted of Quakerism, a crime, in the opinion of her judges, of about equal enormity, and therefore sentenced her to banishment.[117]

The earliest settlers of New England were, for the most part, religious refugees fleeing persecution from European authorities and the Church of England. These refugees saw America, or the "New World" as they would have called it, as an opportunity to create a new society where they could worship their God how they saw fit and be free of religious persecution. During this period, Puritans and Quakers were the predominant religious populations in the northeastern United States. However, there were also Catholics, Jews, Moravians, Scots-Irish Presbyterians, German Pietists, French Huguenots, Jesuits, African religions, African American forms of Christianity, Native American religions and more that were all present in the colonies.[118] The Puritans of New England were known to be pious and intolerant of liberal interpretations of the Bible. Under Puritan rule, women were second-class citizens expected to demonstrate obedience to their husbands and adhere strictly to their religion.[119] However, Mary came from a Quaker community in which women were afforded more public-facing freedoms. For example, Quaker women were able to serve as religious leaders and developed charismatic public personas in their sermons.[120] Puritans were vehemently opposed to many Quaker beliefs and equated practicing the religion to a felony.

The Massachusetts Bay Colony, seated in Boston, publicly executed a Quaker woman named Mary Dyer in 1660. Dyer was an activist who fought to repeal a law that banished Quakers from the colony under threat of death. During her testimony, she stated:

> *I came in obedience to the will of God, the last general court, desiring you to repeal your unrighteous laws of banishment on pain of death; and that same is my work now, and earnest request, although I told you that if you refused to repeal them, the Lord would send others of his servants to witnessed against them.*[121]

Mary Wright Andrews was one of those "other servants of the Lord" who arrived in Boston to demand justice for the execution of Mary Dyer and protest the laws against Quakers. She, along with twenty-seven other Quakers, gave testimony against the unjust Puritan laws and were soon imprisoned by the court.[122] It is here we see that Mary Wright Andrews was likely not an accused witch but rather a convicted Quaker.[123] At eighteen years old, Mary was imprisoned for nearly a year while the court decided what the punishment should be for the group of Quakers. News of Mary Dyer's execution had spread back to England, and the English government

Whipping Quakers at the cart's tail in Boston. *Illustration from Hezekiah Butterworth's* Young Folks' History of Boston *(1881).*

ordered the colony to reduce the severity of the punishment for Quakers.[124] In response, the Massachusetts Bay Colonial court revised the punishment for Quakers so that anyone found guilty "shall be stripped naked from the middle upwards, and tied to a cart's tail, and whipped through the town towards the borders of our jurisdiction, as the warrant shall direct, and so from constable to constable, till they be through any of the outwards towns of our jurisdiction"[125] On May 22, 1661, Mary Wright Andrews and the other twenty-seven prisoners were read the law, and their punishments were carried out. The prisoners were stripped of their clothes and whipped through the streets as they continued to shout out their protest against the corrupt government.[126]

Mary was not the only member of her family to be outspoken and righteous. Mary had two sisters, Lydia and Hannah, who were also emboldened and passionate about the fight for equal rights. Mary's younger sister Hannah Wright traveled to Boston to further address the legal prejudice against Quakers only a year after the release of her sister Mary. The court magistrates did not take Hannah's testimony seriously due to her age. Historian William Sewel commented:

For once a girl of 13 or 14 years of age, called Hannah Wright, whose sister had been banished for religion, was stirred with such zeal, that coming from Long Island some hundreds of miles from Boston, into that bloody town, she appeared in the court there, and warned the magistrates, to spill no more innocent blood. This saying so struck them at first, that all sat silent, till Rawson, the secretary, said "What, shall we be baffled by such a one as this? Come, let us drink a dram!"[127]

Lastly, Mary's youngest sister, Lydia, continued in the Wright family tradition of strong vocal women and traveled to Boston with friend and fellow activist Margaret Brewster in 1677. Margarette Brewster had been ordered to take an oath to the Massachusetts Bay Colony. However, in the Quaker religion, oaths are forbidden for any other purpose besides oaths to God, which Puritan authorities already knew.[128] In protest, Margaret entered the church in Boston with her hair unkempt, barefoot, wearing a sack over her upper garments and her face and hair covered in ash. Naturally, Margaret and her supportive Quaker friends (including Lydia) were arrested. The following is the court transcript from August 4, 1677, in which Lydia testified on behalf of herself and her friend Margaret:

Governor: Call Lydia Wright.
   Clerk: Lydia Wright of Long Island.
   Lydia Wright: Here.
   Governor: Are you one of the women that came in with this woman into Mr. Thatcher's meeting house to disturb him at his worship?
   Lydia Wright: I was, but I disturbed none; for I came in peaceably, and spake not a word to man, woman, or child.
   Governor: What came you for then?
   Lydia Wright: Have you not made a law that we should come to your meeting? For we were peaceably met together at our own meeting house, and for some of your constables came in, and hailed some of our Friends out and said, "This is not a place for you to worship God in." Then we asked him, "Where we should worship God?" Then he said, "We must come to your public worship" And upon the first day following I had something upon my heart to come to your public worship, when we came in peaceably, and spake not a word; yet we were held to prison, and there have been kept near a month.
   S. Bradstreet: Did you come there to hear the Word?
   Lydia Wright: If the word of God was there, I was ready to hear it.
   Governor: Did your parents give consent you come thither?

Lydia Wright: Yes! My Mother did.

Governor: Shew it.

Lydia Wright: If you will stay till I can send home, I will engage to get from under my mother's hand that she gave her consent.

Magistrate Juggins: You are led by the spirit of the Devil to wramble up and down the country, like whores and rogues a cater-wauling [*caterwauling* is a term to describe the act of making a screeching noise like a cat].

Lydia Wright: Such words do not become those who call themselves Christians; for they that sit to judge for God in matters of conscience ought to be sober and serious; for sobriety becomes the People of God; for these are a weighty and ponderous people.

Governor: Did you own this woman?

Lydia Wright: (Yes) I own her, and have unity with her, and I do believe so have all the faithful servants of the Lord, for I know the power and presence of the Lord was with us.

Magistrate Juggins: You are mistaken. You do not know the power of God. You are led by the Spirit and light within you, which is of the Devil; there is but one God and you do (not) worship that God which we worship.

Lydia Wright: I believe thou speakest truth; for if you worshipped that God which we worship, you would not persecute his people; for we worship the God of Abraham, Isaac, and Jacob, and the same God that Daniel worshipped.

...So they cried, "Take her away." [129]

Ultimately, the Massachusetts Bay court sentenced her to the same punishment that her sister Mary received seven years prior. She was to be stripped naked, tied to a cart and to whipped through town.[130] Lydia returned to her family home in Oyster Bay—near the present-day Theodore Roosevelt Elementary School—after her punishment had been carried out. Lydia kept fighting for Quaker rights and even traveled to Barbados to continue her mission, where she eventually died in 1682 at twenty-seven years old.[131] The middle sister, Hannah, met a similar fate while traveling in Virginia to meet with the Quaker colony there. Hannah died there from drowning at the age of twenty-nine.[132] Mary Wright, however, married Samuel Andrews of her hometown in Oyster Bay, where they sold their land and moved to Mansfield Township, Burlington County, New Jersey, and had many children.[133] The couple are likely buried in Mansfield Cemetery on Route 206. This case is particularly interesting, as there is a

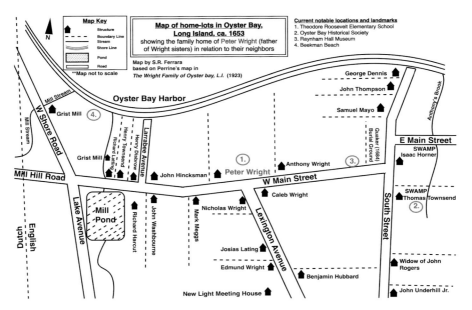

Above: Map of Oyster Bay in 1650s indicating home lot of Peter Wright, father of the three Wright sisters. *Courtesy of author, based on Perrine (1923).*

Opposite: *The Three Witches from Macbeth* by Henry Fuseli (1741–1825). *The New York Public Library Digital Collections.*

recurring theme of three female sisters such as the Moirai (or Three Fates) in ancient witch folklore, not too dissimilar to the three Wright sisters in this seventeenth-century account. However, the three sisters were not accused of satanic witchcraft, only of Quakerism and activism.

It is unlikely that Mary Wright Andrews was accused or tried for witchcraft during her lifetime over 350 years ago. However, she has posthumously been discussed as a potential accused witch. Mary Wright Andrews may be the origin of the Mary's Grave legend, as her myth persists as the "Witch of Oyster Bay." However, Mary is a given name commonly found throughout the genealogies of Long Island families, and it is impossible to definitively connect her to the Mary's Grave story. For example, one Mary Hall was accused of witchcraft in Setauket as was a Mary Newton in Oakdale, discussed later. Though there are different versions of the local Mary's Grave folklore, a common version argues that Mary was a witch who tortured animals, may have been abused herself and lived in one of the towns along the north shore of Long Island. Besides living in a north shore town, these attributes seem to be unlikely for Mary Wright Andrews. If she is the namesake for the local legend, then the attributes were added to her story at a later time to scare and intimidate teenagers in the area who dare explore remote locations reported to be her unmarked grave. This is a common rite of passage for teenagers in this area. In reality, Mary was quite the opposite of  a cynical, tortured victim who might haunt her home and wreak havoc. In fact, she was a staunch feminist and activist who was quick to react to injustices toward women within a patriarchal government and was further empowered by her two sisters who supported her and her efforts, even if it meant imprisonment. What's known for certain is that all three Wright sisters liked to serve back some trouble to the cozy male magistrates of Puritan New England.

7

THE HARTFORD HYSTERIA

Judith Varleth Bayard and Goodwife Ayres

New England was certainly a hostile environment for women during the seventeenth century. Witchcraft accusations were frequent through New England villages, and women were not only accused but also executed. The men who defended these accused women met similar fates. Religious beliefs made them susceptible to supernatural fears of their day and the contemporary doctrines that discussed the existence and extermination of witches in society. For accused women, it was nearly impossible to escape a government that was suffused with prejudice and paranoia. Fortunately for some, the English government in New York had varying relations with the colonies in Connecticut and Massachusetts. These shifting relations with New York made it possible for accused witches to escape accusations and trials in New England and flee to villages in New York to seek shelter. The first recorded Europeans to flee the theocratic governments of New England and seek refuge in New York were Judith Varleth Bayard and possibly Goodwife Ayres, who were both accused in 1662 during a witch hunt in Hartford, Connecticut. Judith Varleth Bayard was saved from her trial by the direct intervention of New York governor Petrus Stuyvesant, a family friend. However, Goodwife Ayres escaped trial with her husband, William, and it is only suspected that she decamped to New York, though varying accounts also place her in Rhode Island.

The stories of Judith Varleth Bayard and Goodwife Ayres may end in New York, but their connection with witchcraft began in nearby Connecticut.

In March 1662, eight-year-old Elizabeth Kelly demonstrated symptoms of a terrible sickness, worrying her parents greatly. Healthcare during this period was relatively undeveloped for European frontiersmen, and religious prayer was one method used to combat diseases thought to be caused by evil forces. These beliefs were supported when young Elizabeth cried out in pain, speaking of an invisible malevolent force, "Father! Father! Help me! Goodwife Ayres is upon me, she chokes me, she kneels on my belly. She will break my bowels. She pinches me. She will make me black and blue."[134] Elizabeth ultimately succumbed to her sickness, leaving her parents behind to accuse Goodwife Ayres of bewitching their daughter. After all, their daughter had visited Goodwife Ayres just a day earlier and shared hot broth from the same bowl. Authorities promptly arrested Ayres and sent for surgeon Bryan Rosseter to perform what would later be considered the first forensic autopsy in American

A bewitched woman vomiting. Woodcut. 1720. *Wellcome Collection.*

history.[135] However, Rosseter arrived at Hartford five days after the death and misattributed natural phases of decomposition to supernatural causes. Modern interpretation of Elizabeth's symptoms, such as hallucinations, bruising, foul odor, a red spot on her face and so on, indicates that she suffered from sepsis-caused delirium, achalasia (contraction of the esophagus) and ultimately pneumonia.[136] Luckily, Goodwife Ayres and her husband escaped prison and potential execution by fleeing the colony early in the investigation.

Hartford had quickly succumbed to hysteria at the thought of neighborly bewitchment. A young girl named Ann Cole furthered the townsfolk's paranoia by demonstrating demonic possession and speaking in tongues. Ann claimed that a "company of familiars of the evil one" had claimed her body and devised ways they would "afflict her body, spoile her name, [and] hinder her marriage."[137] Ann had resorted to speaking in a Dutch accent during her performance and ultimately named her neighbor Rebecca Greensmith as the witch responsible for her bewitchment.

Rebecca Greensmith was a seemingly appropriate and believable target for Ann Cole's accusation. After all, she was an older woman, had been married three times in her life and already had a tarnished reputation. Rebecca Greensmith was married to Nathaniel Greensmith during this time, and historical records indicate that the couple had a reputation for causing trouble. Nathaniel had been fined for battery and theft on numerous occasions, while Rebecca was thought of as a "lewd, ignorant, and considerably aged woman" by the town's pastor.[138] Rebecca confessed to her crimes, but we do not know the motives behind her confession or what forms of interrogation were used to gain her admission of guilt. However, after Rebecca's confession, her husband quickly abandoned her; she returned the favor in her second confession.

Here follows Rebecca Greensmith's testimony, with some text replaced to correct for spelling or grammar:[139]

Rebecca Greensmith testifies in Court January 8, 1663.

1. That my husband on Friday night last when I came to prison told me that "now thou hast confessed against thyself, leave me alone and say nothing of me and I will be good unto thy children."

2. I do now testify that formerly when my husband had told me of his great travel and labor I wondered at...how he did it...before I was married and when I was married I asked him how he did it, and he answered me he had help that I knew not of.

3. About three years ago as I think it: my husband and I were in the wood several miles from home and were looking for a pig that we lost and I saw a creature, a red creature, following my husband and when I came to him I asked him what it was that was with him and he told me it was a fox.

4. Another time when he and I drove our hogs into the woods beyond the pound that was to keep young cattle several miles off I went before the hogs to call them and looking back I saw two creatures like dogs, one a little blacker than the other, they came after my husband pretty close to him and one did seem to me to touch him I asked him what they were he told me he thought foxes I was still afraid when I saw anything because I heard so much of him before I married him.

5. I have seen logs that my husband had brought home in his cart that I wondered at it that he could get them into the cart being a man of little body and weak to my apprehension and the logs were such that I thought two men such as he could not have done it. I speak all this out of love to my husband's soul and it is much against my will that I am now necessitated to speak against my husband, I desire that the Lord would open his heart to own and speak the truth.

6. I also testify that I, being in the wood, at a meeting there was with me Goody Seager, Goodwife Sandford & Goodwife Ayres; and at another time there was a meeting under a tree in the green by our house & there was there James Walkely, Peter Grants wife, Goodwife Ayres, & Henry Palmers wife of Wethersfield, & Goody Seager, & there we danced, & had a bottle of sack: it was in the night & something like a cat called me out to the meeting & I was in Mr. Varlets orchard with Mrs. Judith Varlett [Varleth] & she told me that she was much troubled with the Marshall Jonath: Gilbert & cried, & she said if it lay in her power she would do him a mischief, or what hurt she could.

Rebecca Greensmith named Judith Varleth in her confession, and shortly after, authorities had Judith detained. Luckily for Judith, her family connections saved her from possible execution. Peter Stuyvesant ultimately agreed to help and wrote a letter to the magistrates at Hartford for the release of Judith, which reads as follows:

Honored & Worthy Sirs

By this occasion of my brother in law (being necessitated to make a second voyage for aide of his distressed sister Judith Varleth imprisoned as we

are informed upon pretend accusation off witchery, we really believe &
out her known education, life conversation & profession off faith we dear
assure, that she is innocent of such a horrible crime & therefore I doubt
not he [Nicholas] will now as formerly find your honors favor & aide for
the Innocent) I cannot omit to acquaint you (which should be done sooner
if my absence had not hindered it) that one John Younge, whether upon
your orders (as he pretends) I doubt, had undertaken as by his seditious
letters may appear to divert & revoke the English towns in this province
under the protection of the high and mighty Lords, the Estates General of
the United Belgick Provinces and in the jurisdiction of the right honorable
Lords of the West India Company settled, off their oath & due obedience
unto us their lawful governor, which his unlawful proceedings, amongst
the silly & common people, without any acknowledgement or addresses
unto us as governor of this province, if you will known as we do not
hope, yow may take notice that is an absolute breach & a nullification
of the agreement about the Limits 1650 made at Hartford between the
honorable commissioners of New England & us as Governor General of
this province & that by that means the aforementioned high and mighty
Lords the Estates General & the right honorable Lords of the West
India Company were given just grounds & reasons to demand & by such
means as they in wisdom shall think me to recover all that tract of land
between Greenwich & the fresh River, so long unjustly as it now doeth
appear, without any patent or commission possessed & detained from the
aforementioned first possessors & owners, whereof the monument off
the house the Hope, by commission of the aforesaid Lords built and
without molestation upon the fresh and Connecticut River possessed many
years, before any off the English nation did come there. But confiding
& trusting more in the words & promises of the honorable Governor
Winthrop, as he did depart from hence, we shall with more discretion
expect his deserved arrival & leave the matters to our superiors in Europe
& shall after my respects love & service presented, expect with the bearer
your categorical answer over and about the aforementioned John Youngs
seditious doings & remain

Amsterdam in New Netherland   Your loving friend & neighbor
the 13th of Xbre 1662.   P. Stuyvesant.[140]

Petrus Stuyvesant. *Wikimedia Commons / Public domain.*

After the Hartford magistrates received Stuyvesant's letter, Judith was released and fled to New York. Judith married Nicholas Bayard some years later, and the couple settled on Hooge Stratt (High Street), Manhattan, New York. The fear of witches seemed to have affected English settlers far more frequently than the Dutch residing in New Netherland. In fact, Governor Petrus Stuyvesant, in an attempt to coax English settlers into the New Haven Colony (present-day Newark, New Jersey), offered impunity to any charges of witchcraft under his government so that anyone convicted of witchcraft would not face the death penalty.[141] His proposition reads as follows:

Concerning the appeals, it is hereby granted and confirmed that all capital sentences wherein the parties are convinced by own confession, shall be put in execution by the court of courts without appeal, but in dark and dubious matters, especially witchcraft, such sentences of death shall not be put in execution, as with approbation of the Governor General and council in time being.[142]

This weighty declaration marked yet another step toward making New York a sanctuary for those who would be otherwise senselessly killed by their fearful neighbors.

8

MARY HALL AND RALPH HALL

On Christmas Day 1664, a tavern keeper named George Wood dropped dead of some unknown cause lost to the pages of history. Wood left behind a widow by the name of Ann Rogers, whose infant also succumbed to some unknown malady and died shortly after George. Over and into the next year, suspicion built around local couple Mary and Ralph Hall, both of whom were surrounded by gossip and rumors from their suspicious neighbors, with tales of sorcery and secret pacts between the Halls and the devil himself. Ralph and Mary were arrested, and on October 2, 1665, they were charged with crimes of murder by way of witchcraft for the deaths of George Wood and the infant child of Ann Rogers.

Mary and Ralph Hall lived in the town of Seatallcott, East Riding, of Yorkshire, Long Island (present-day Setauket, town of Brookhaven, Suffolk County). Mary Hall was likely an older woman, perhaps of middle age, and may have had a reputation as an herbal healer within Seatallcott.[143] As we know from Elizabeth Garlick's case, middle-aged individuals were particularly vulnerable targets for witchcraft accusations. Her husband, Ralph, was a landowner, at least for a short while, in Seatallcott. The couple had left Connecticut and arrived in Seatallcott sometime in late 1664[144] and were permitted a land plot early the following year on February 25, 1665.[145] Mary quickly fell victim to slander, with one Mr. Smith (likely Richard "Bull" Smith of Smithtown) being sued for a defamation complaint by the Halls and ordered to pay her five marks.[146]

The magistrates having considered the complaints of Hall and his wife against Mr. Smith, do judge the said Mr. Smith hath not sufficiently made good what he hath said of her, and therefore Mr. Smith is ordered to pay the woman five marks.
June 9th, 1664 [147]

Mr. Smith's statement was never recorded, and we do not know what exactly was said against Mary Hall.

The victim, George Wood, was a tavern keeper who suffered from some unknown prolonged illness that Mary may have attempted to treat with herbal remedies.[148] George Wood did not have the easiest life before his demise. Having started on Long Island in Southold, he was banished for "not being fit to live among them."[149] He then moved to East Hampton and fell into indentured servitude for several masters—Lion Gardiner, Stephen Goodyear and others—though soon found himself accused of lying, stealing and adultery, having fathered a child with an Indian woman.[150] After moving with his family to Seatallcott, he was permitted to open the first ordinary (tavern). After his death, George Wood's widow, Ann, married a man named Henry Rogers,[151] possibly while she was pregnant with George's child. However, Barstow argues that the notorious adventurer Captain John Scott took in "a wench on widow Rogers and kept her in the house with his wife and had a child by her, a girl," as stated by witness Francis Lovelace.[152] In a book review, historian and regional expert John Strong speculates that the likelihood of two "widow Rogers" in Seatallcott at this time seems unlikely and also aligns with the reputed behavior of John Scott,[153] though he argues that more documentation is needed to support this claim and that he remains skeptical. Regardless of who the actual father was, Ann Rogers's infant also succumbed to some unknown illness. Though we know the Halls were new to Seatallcott at this time, we do not know the details of what terrible gossip surrounded them and how the rumors perpetuated into their eventual arrest and trial. Nor can we authenticate the herbal interests and proficiencies of Mary that differed from any other seventeenth-century settler woman. Their lives, as we know them now, can be reconstructed from town property records and the recorded proceedings of their trial:

The Constable and Overseer of the town of Seatallcott, in the East Riding of Yorkshire upon Long Island, Do present for our sovereign Lord, the King that Ralph Hall of Seatallcott aforesaid, upon this 25th day of December; being Christmas day last, was twelve months in the 15th

year of the reign of our sovereign Lord Charles the second, by the grace
of God, King of England, Scotland, France, and Ireland, defender of
the faith etc., and several other days and times since that day, by some
detestable and wicked arts commonly called witchcraft and sorcery did
(as in suspected) maliciously and feloniously, practice and exercise at the
said town of Seatallcott in the East Riding of Yorkshire on Long Island
aforesaid on the person of George Wood, late of the same place by which
wicked and detestable arts, that said George Wood (as is suspected) most
dangerously and mortally sickened and languished, and not long after by
the aforesaid wicked and detestable arts, that said George Wood (as in
likewise suspected) died.

Moreover, the Constable and overseers of the said Towne of Seatallcott,
in the East Riding of Yorkshire upon Long Island aforesaid, do further
present for our sovereign Lord the King, that some while after the death
of the aforesaid George Wood, the said Ralph Hall did (as is suspected)
divers times by the wicked and detestable arts, commonly called witchcraft
and sorcery, maliciously and feloniously practice and exercise at the said
town of Seatallcott, in the East Riding of Yorkshire upon Long Island
aforesaid, on the person of an infant child of Ann Rogers, widow of the
aforesaid George Wood deceased, by who wicked and detestable arts, the
said infant child (as is suspected) most dangerously and morally sickened
and languished, and not long after by the said wicked and detestable arts
(as likewise suspected) died, and so the said Constable and Overseers do
present, that the said George Wood, and the said infant said child, by the
ways and means aforesaid, most wickedly maliciously and feloniously were
(as is suspected) murdered by the said Ralph Hall at the times and places
aforesaid, against the peace of our sovereign lord the King and against the
laws of the government in such cases provided.
Court of Assizes, New York
October 2nd, 1665 [154]

This indictment was then read for Mary Hall, with the same charges against her; both Mary and Ralph pleaded not guilty. The grand jury for this case was composed of reputable and distinguished men from the surrounding settlements: Thomas Baker of East Hampton[155] (foreman of the jury), Captain John Seamans of Hempstead, Mr. Hallet[156] and Anthony Waters of Jamaica, Thomas Wandall of Marshpath Kills, Mr. Nicolls of Stamford and Balthazar de Haart, John Garland, Jacob Leisler, Antonio de Mill, Alexander Munro and Thomas Searle of New York.[157] After some deliberation, the jury found the couple not guilty, although they did not completely absolve Mary Hall. Their decision read as follows:

> *We having seriously considered the case committed to our charge, against the prisoners at the bar, and having well weighed the evidence, we find that there are some suspicions by the evidence, of what the women is charged with, but nothing considerable of value to take away her life. But in reference to the man we find nothing considerable to charge with him with.*[158]

As expected for the period, Ralph Hall was acquitted of all charges, but his wife, Mary Hall, still had some authorities suspicious. As Mary was still under some suspicion, Ralph was ordered to pay the court every year for her appearance at every court session as long as they were to live within the same jurisdiction. The court records are limited, and we do not know what swayed the jury, but while witness testimony was read, there were no in-person witnesses present, which likely favored the Halls' case for innocence.

After their release, the Hall family moved to Minneford Island (now City Island, Bronx) just east off the coast of Manhattan. They were welcomed by the owner of the island, Thomas Pell, who most likely felt guilty for his family's involvement in the witchcraft trial and execution of Goody Knapp in 1653.[159] Then on August 21, 1668, New York colonial governor Richard Nicolls released Mary Hall of her appearance obligations, arguing that there had been no further incidents of accusations against them since the hearing and no need to further suspect her of witchcraft.[160] This case likely received minor attention, as it was overshadowed by larger events such as the English wresting control of the New Netherland colony from the Dutch Empire in 1664. Under the reign of James, Duke of York, the English captured the Dutch colony in a surprise attack and changed its name from New Netherland to New York, marking this case, technically, as the first witch trial in New York, concurrent with the start of the Second Anglo-Dutch War.

Pinpointing the area where the Hall family lived in Setauket is a difficult but potentially accomplishable task. From property records, we know Ralph Hall purchased ten acres of land in "Nonamaset,"[161] an area in Setauket that has yet to be identified. This term was identified in William Wallace Tooker's *The Indian Place Names on Long Island*.[162] If we are to cautiously use Tooker's translations then the Algonquian place name Nonamaset, also spelled Nanemoset, may refer to a "brook or creek of uncertain location" or "at or, about the fishing spot."[163] Further, Nanemoset is also referenced in a December 5, 1663 land deed by John Scott detailing an area of land "bounded easterly with Nanemoset Brook, westerly with Nessaquague east line, and running south to the middle of the island, even to the said Indian's utmost bounds, and north to the Sound."[164] This information may place the Halls' home lot on western Strong's Neck, closest to a waterway, likely along the east bank of the channel running south from Conscience Bay.

Hall also had five acres "in the Little Neck" by "Shoemakers Point" by the "rock at the neck."[165] The area called Little Neck in now known as Strong's Neck.[166] The simple description of "the rock" as a landmark could reference numerous glacial erratics found on the north shore of Long Island, some even long displaced by more recent development. In the Setauket area, there are two extant boulders that may reference the mentioned landmark. One is known as "Patriot Rock," located on Main Street between Dyke Road and Old Field Road, the other is known as "Indian Rock," located on Main Street between Lake Street and Watson Lane. However, if either of these could even classify as the mentioned rock, then several contextual clues lean closer to Patriots Rock since the deed record states that Hall is to "do half the water fence by the rock at the neck."[167] A water fence is a term that describes "artificial ditches and wooden fences that extend into waterways."[168] Patriots Rock is closer to the channel on the west side of the neck that connects to Conscience Bay, the local waterway. Shoemakers Point, based on various mentions in town records,[169] may be identifiable by land plot reconstruction and contextual clues.

After the Halls moved to City Island, Ralph Hall sold his home to Alexander Briant, who then sold the property to Evan Salisberry of Brookhaven on August 23, 1665.[170] By December 3, 1668, a Mr. Lane was living at this location and exchanged with Samuel Ackerly. The Halls may have lived out the rest of their days on City Island, in the Bronx, although a 1673 tax assessment lists a "Ralph Haull" in Hempstead, Long Island, and an inventory of their property indicates they continued to live a modest life.[171] The couple were never formerly accused of witchcraft again, though we may never know what the rest of their lives entailed and what gossip persisted to haunt them.

9

KATHERINE HARRISON

The Puritan society of seventeenth-century New England limited the public agency of women in daily life. Women were restrained to a second-class status during this time, and many of the theological and legal systems were designed to ensure woman remained subservient to men. This period was bleak for women, and there were only so many avenues in which they could express themselves or retain any semblance of social power. Power and agency were not something that women could easily obtain by themselves—it most often had to be bestowed. For Katherine Harrison of Wethersfield, Connecticut, being a healer was her attempt at creating a unique identity in a world working against her. However, she did not retain real social power until after the death of her husband, John Harrison, whose large estate she inherited. In fact, the large inheritance that John Harrison left behind made Katherine one of the wealthiest landowners in her community, and within the patriarchal society of seventeenth-century Connecticut, this was socially unacceptable. Widows were expected to remarry in order to maintain a male figure as the head of the household. Katherine's decision not to remarry, along with her proclaimed esoteric knowledge, made her a target, as she was formally accused of witchcraft after two years of being a widow. However, there are always more details to a good story, and it should be noted here at the beginning that, like most accused women, Katherine had plenty of issues with her neighbors from her earliest arrival in the community. She is reported to have been rather disagreeable, making her all the more interesting. Katherine's story bleeds into New York history as she moved to the town of Westchester, where she was, once more, accused of being a witch and frightening the Westchester community (present-day Westchester Square in the Bronx).[172]

The lives of women accused of witchcraft were not well documented, as is the case for many accused women in this book. However, the Harrison case is unique: many of the witness testimonies from her trial in Connecticut still exist. Through these witness testimonies—supplemented with town records, genealogical records and some understanding[173] of women's lives in the seventeenth century—we are able to reconstruct the "middle third" part of Katherine Harrison's life to some extent.[174] Further, the Harrison case set a precedent in colonial legal history concerning the use and legitimacy of witnesses and spectral evidence in the proceedings of witchcraft cases. For the first time, Connecticut magistrates were confronted with difficult questions regarding the legal and theological definitions of matters and events concerning the occult and diabolical witchcraft. The results of this case rippled through history and would later affect the proceedings of future witchcraft cases in the colonies.

But first, let us dive into what we know about Katherine Harrison. It is accepted by historians that Katherine Harrison came from England (town unknown) to Hartford, Connecticut, in 1651.[175] As a person of lower social status, she spent her first years (1651–53) in America working as a house servant for the wealthy merchant Captain John Cullick.[176] It was during these initial years in Hartford that she developed a reputation and dislike from her fellow house servants, who would years later testify against her during her witch trials. Katherine wanted to be unique, so she would insert herself into dramatic household situations with self-promoted abilities as a healer and a fortune teller. Rumors and gossip that orbited Katherine included notions that claimed she was a sabbath breaker, a notorious liar and a prostitute who "would follow the army in England"; she performed feats of great strength unbecoming of her abilities and enjoyed fortune telling with suspicious accuracy.[177] Witnesses later testified that she boasted about her familiarity and/or tutelage under famed English astrologer William Lilly and that this knowledge gave her predictions credibility.[178] Katherine made several mentions of William Lilly and was reported to have "read from his book," likely his most popular work, *Christian Astrology Modestly Treated of in Three Books* (1659).[179]

Katherine appeared in Wethersfield in May 1653, married to a local, John Harrison, and had three daughters with him in a short period.[180] However, Katherine aroused suspicions after her arrival in Connecticut with her self-promoted fortune-telling and healer's knowledge. When she left Hartford and arrived in Wethersfield, she likely was suspected of being a witch from day one.[181] The fact that Katherine had three daughters may have even added to suspicions of her witchy guilt, as three women are reminiscent of the three fates in Greek mythology later represented by the witches of Shakespearian lore. Katherine Harrison's husband, John Harrison of Wethersfield, died in 1666, leaving behind a large estate.[182] When John unexpectedly died, she was no longer protected from neighborly rumors, now turned into public accusations.

John Harrison's ubiquity in history is described as "strangely elusive," as he briefly served in different minor elected offices of little notoriety such as town crier, fence viewer, surveyor and constable, though not as frequently as was expected of men of wealth during this period.[183] John Putnam Demos argues that John likely came from a relatively humble background; married Katherine, who also came from few economic resources; and together through resourcefulness built a considerable financial estate. This type of social mobility was rare and could easily have contributed to their neighbors' collective resentment toward them.[184] Further, Katherine's shrewd but disagreeable nature often worked against her attempts at providing local healthcare to her neighbors, in what some would call poor bedside manners. Nevertheless, on several occasions Katherine is recorded as attempting to aid her ill neighbors. In one instance, she dressed the wound of an unidentified man's big toe;[185] another time, Katherine helped a neighbor with "diet, drink, and plasters."[186] Katherine's home remedies of "diet, drink, and plasters" offer us a unique insight in her life and her contemporary approaches to healthcare. In many circumstances of illness and injury, European settlers relied on a number of topical medical approaches, namely, oils, ointments and plasters. The difference between the three materials was mainly viscosity.[187] Oils are a more liquid substance and may relieve issues temporarily, with the substance being absorbed or dissipating quickly. Ointments, like creams, are thicker and easier to spread and contain and could remain on the afflicted spot for a longer period of time. Plasters are the stickiest of the substances and take the longest sustained amount of time to be absorbed and remedy the affected area. All three substances would have been available in any apothecary or known to local healers, as they are constructed from natural ingredients such as animal parts, flowers, herbs and common minerals.[188]

Katherine was first accused in April 1668, and her witchcraft crimes fall into four categories as laid out by scholar Walter Woodward:[189] injury and

A man removing a plaster from his hand. Etching attributed to David Teniers (1610–1690). *Wellcome Collection.*

murder by magic, fortune-telling, spectral appearance or shape-shifting and supernatural meddling (referred to as "harms"). All four categories imply a direct connection between the accused (Harrison) and the devil. Injury and murder by magic describes homicidal intent through the inappropriate use of herbal or folk medicine, employing one's apparition to attack a victim or cursing a victim to physical injury. Fortune-telling describes the act of receiving information from the devil about future events and employing or relaying that information to others. Early settlers generally accepted some forms of astrology that could aid in cultivation and harvesting but considered the foretelling of future events as taboo or evil. Spectral appearance is similar to the idea of astral projection, though in this context, it was a talent that could be bestowed on an individual after making a pact with the devil. Spectral appearance included the ability to project one's spirit in the form of an apparition and cause mayhem. Lastly, "to do harms" implied the attribution of unfamiliar medical symptoms (for example, stiff limbs or nose bleeds) or daily common misfortunes (spoiled food or drink, weird animal behavior, startling home accidents and so on) as a result of an individual, who, by powers given to them by the devil, could wreak havoc from afar. Harms could also include perceived supernatural abilities of those who are accused or abilities that seem too advanced and skillful to be natural. In all categories of witchcraft crime, a direct relationship with the devil was implied.

The witnesses who testified against Katherine refer to one or more of these categories as evidence of what they perceived as diabolical witchcraft. These witnesses included John Wells, Elizabeth Smith, Mary Olcott, John Graves, Thomas Bracey, Thomas Waples, Goodwife Johnson, Joan Francis, William Warren, Mary Hale, Samuel Martin, Eleazar Kinnerly, Rebecca Smith, Richard Montague and Alice Wakely.[190]

INJURY AND MURDER BY MAGIC

Goodwife Johnson's testimony related to the injuries of her husband, Jacob Johnson, caused by Katherine Harrison. In her testimony, Jacob was employed by Katherine's husband, John Harrison, to pick up a load of meal from Windsor, Connecticut, by canoe. Jacob returned ill and was treated by Katherine with "diet, drink, and plasters." However, this treatment was ineffective, and the Johnson family sent for another individual, Captain Atwood, for help. Presumably, this aggravated Katherine Harrison. That same night, Goodwife Johnson claimed to have seen the apparition of Katherine looking at her ill husband, Jacob, at which point Jacob's nose began to bleed.[191] Eleazar Kinnerly's testimony related to the fact that he and his wife felt Katherine bewitched Eleazar's in-laws, the Robbins family. When Eleazar's father-in-law, Mr. Robbins, passed away, Katherine used the phrasing "when your father was *killed*," implying murder when there was no reason to suspect foul play. With the context of the witchcraft trial, Katherine referring to the death in this manner aroused suspicion. Eleazar also presumed that his mother-in-law was bewitched in her sickness.[192] Alice Wakely testified further to the bewitchment of the Robbinses, stating that Mrs. Robbins, at the time before her death, had stiff and immoveable limbs; after death, she was suspiciously limber.[193]

Rebecca Smith testified first on the behalf of Goodwife Gilbert, who owned a black hat and let Katherine borrow said hat. Katherine offered to buy the hat from Goodwife Gilbert, but she refused to sell. From then on, when Goodwife Gilbert wore the hat, she experienced terrible pains, but only when wearing the hat. It was decided to cast the hat into the fire. Further, Rebecca Smith stated that her thighs and legs would stiffen often, and she would feel sick, to the point that others suspected she was bewitched. However, Rebecca—being seventy-five years old—did admit this could be common ailments of old age.[194] Joan Francis testified that the night before her child was stricken fatally ill, the apparition of Katherine Harrison appeared. The child was sick for three weeks and a day, then passed away.[195] Mary Hale gave a particularly righteous testimony, concerning her triumphant battles against a maleficent entity that had the body of a dog and the head of Katherine Harrison. The first night the creature attacked, Mary had a good fire going so that the whole room was illuminated. As she lay in bed, she heard a startling noise come from inside the room. Then, a heavy thing fell on her legs with tremendous force, slowly making its way up until it was pressing on her chest, making it difficult to breathe. Mary then claims she identified the dog body with Katherine's head. However, Katherine was in jail awaiting her witchcraft trial. The creature jumped off of her, paced the floors, walked to her father's bedside, then disappeared. The next night it happened, the creature followed the same pattern, first jumping on the legs, then compressing the chest. Mary said the room was dark during the second encounter, but she felt the face of the creature with her hands, and it felt like a woman's. After feeling the face of the creature, her fingers were injured and bruised by the morning. The next night the creature appeared, Mary tried to call out to her father but could not wake her parents until the creature vanished. Finally, during the creature's last appearance, Mary had attempted to call out to her parents to no avail. The creature said to her, "You said that I would not come again, but are you not afraid of me?" To which Mary replied, "No." The creature replied, "I will make you afraid of me before I am done with you," then proceeded to

The Nightmare (1781) by Henry Fuseli. *Wikimedia Commons / Public domain.*

crush Mary. Mary tried to call out to her parents, but they could not hear her. The creature said, "Though you do call, they shall not hear, till I am gone....You said I have preserved my cart to carry me to the gallows, but to you, I will make it a death cart" Mary remarked that she spoke similar words to her sister privately, presumably about Katherine Harrison. Mary replied, "I fear not, because God will keep me." The creature then said, "I have commission to kill you, Mary." Mary replied, "Who gave you commission?" The creature said, "God did." Mary exclaimed, "The Devil is a liar from the very beginning for God will not give commission to murder, therefore it must be from the Devil." The creature then pressed on her chest harder and, in pathetic defeat, said, "You will make these events known broad, but if you keep it a secret, I will come no longer to afflict you." Mary replied, "I will make this known broad." Mary then stated that she thought the creature's voice was that of Katherine Harrison and affirmed that the whole story was true.

FORTUNE-TELLING

Thomas Waples described Katherine as a "noted liar who read Mr. Lilly's book in England."[196] Samuel Martin testified that in March 1669, he was at Katherine's house and she predicted the death of Josiah Willard and Samuel Hale Sr. and that Willard would go first because he was sick and could no longer speak.[197] Fellow servant William Warren later testified that, during their time together as servants in Captain Cullick's home, Katherine was a fortune-teller and "looked upon my hands," implying chiromancy or palmistry, and learned this practice from William Lilly back in England.[198] Two others of Katherine's contemporaries at the Cullick home testified to a more dramatic incident. Elizabeth Smith née Bateman[199] testified that during their time together as servants, Katherine was a "great or notorious liar, a sabbath breaker, and one who told fortunes."[200] Elizabeth claimed that Katherine foretold she would be married to a Simon, which came to fruition when Elizabeth married Simon Smith. However, Mary Olcott's testimony offers some more clarity into the controversy. Olcott testified that during their time as servants, Elizabeth was involved with a man named William Chapman, so much so that their peers thought they would soon be married. However, from court records, we know that on March 2, 1654, Captain Cullick issued a complaint against William Chapman for trying to marry Elizabeth Bateman without permission from Captain Cullick, their master.[201] The courts decided in favor of Captain Cullick and fined Chapman five pounds and to serve fourteen days in jail. Fellow servants Thomas Waples and William Warren were found to be "accessories to the disorder." It appeared that Katherine Harrison was acting on the behalf of Captain Cullick to influence her fellow servants' emotions and break up Elizabeth and William's dalliance.[202] After the breakup, Elizabeth married local Simon Smith, thus fulfilling the foretelling by Katherine. This meddling was likely transparent after the fact and certainly may have disturbed Elizabeth Smith. Perhaps this is the cause of her heated testimony against Katherine as a "great or notorious liar."[203] Regardless, it is important to note here that Katherine's fortune-telling abilities were self-promoted, be she a liar or not, and Katherine justified her abilities based on her tutelage under (or reading of) William Lilly, a popular astrologer in England during the period, and not from an obvious connection to the devil.

Spectral Appearance and Shape-Shifting

Mary Hale and Joan Francis weren't the only ones to report seeing the spectral appearance of Katherine Harrison. Thirty-one-year-old Thomas Bracy also testified that he had witnessed Katherine's apparition on different occasions. Bracy claimed that Katherine Harrison, along with James Wakley,[204] appeared at his bedside as apparitions and bickered over how they were to kill Thomas. James suggested they cut out Thomas's throat, while Katherine argued for strangulation. Katherine's spirit then pounced on Thomas to strangle him, pulling at him and pinching the "flesh…from his bones." The next day, Thomas's parents discovered him to be bruised. Contextual evidence seems to imply Thomas was much younger during this incident, relaying that he shared a bed with his siblings during this aforementioned event. Then another time, Thomas was visiting Sergeant Hugh Wells at his house, across the street from the Harrison family. Thomas witnessed a cart traveling toward the Harrisons' house loaded with hay and a red calf's head sitting on top with ears standing straight up. Thomas watched the calf's head all the way until the cart reached the Harrison's barn, at which point the calf vanished and Katherine Harrison stood up in its place. Thomas ran over and, "giving out words," accused Katherine of witchcraft, to which Katherine became angry and stated she would get even with Thomas.[205]

Harms

Lastly, five individuals—John Wells, Thomas Waples, Richard Montague, John Graves and Joan Francis—mentioned various harms caused by Katherine Harrison in their testimonies. John Wells testified that seven or eight years earlier, he was sent by his mother to retrieve their cows that had wandered. Having spotted the cows, John Wells crossed the street, but his legs had become locked in place, preventing him from reaching his herd. He witnessed Katherine Harrison rise up from behind one of his cows with a bucket in her hand and run back toward her house, presumably with stolen milk. As soon as she was out of sight, John regained the use of his legs.[206] Thomas Waples, in his testimony, included that during his time as a servant alongside Katherine Harrison, she was able to spin thread at unusual and likely supernatural rates.[207] Similarly, Richard Montague testified that Katherine told him of her bees that had flown away from her house a great distance but that she was able to retrieve the bees in a suspiciously short period of time.[208] In Joan Francis's testimony, Katherine's daughter came by to ask if she had any beer to spare, but Joan was all out. Shortly after, Joan began to brew more beer, and the head of the barrel shot off as if pressurized and flew across the room, shooting out the hops along with it. Joan noted that the barrel was not bunged off, implying that the barrel could not have been pressurized to cause such an effect. Further, Joan claimed it was a new barrel she had just received from Joseph Wright. The event was so dramatic that it frightened her children. Then, in front of the fireplace, Katherine Harrison briefly appeared, staring at Joan, silhouetted by the light of the flames.[209] John Graves testified that he heard the Harrison family might be witches and decided to let his oxen graze on their land to see if anything weird would happen. He tied the oxen to his cart and led them to go feed. However, they would not graze and stood staring. He then witnessed his knots become untied on their own and fall to the ground, freeing the cattle. He quickly retied the ropes and once more attempted to let the oxen graze, but they suddenly became frightened and violently ran away, breaking the ropes. He claimed to have never had this issue with his oxen grazing in other areas.[210]

During the course of these testimonies, Katherine wasted no time making counterclaims for the injuries she had sustained by her neighbors. Some of the townsfolk decided to torment Katherine by destroying or harming her property. From Katherine's testimony, it would seem she knew who among her neighbors was responsible but perhaps refrained from specific identification so as not to further add to the excitement and hostility within the town.[211] Her testimony reads as follows:

> *May it please this honored court to have patience with me a little; having none to complain to, but the fathers of the Commonwealth; and yet meeting with many injuries; which necessitates me, to look out for some relief; I am bold to present you with those few lines; as a relation of the wrongs that I suffer, humbly craving your serious consideration of my state a widow, of my wrongs (which I conceive) are great, and that as far as the rules of justice and equity will allow, I may have right and do recompense; that what I would present to you in the first place is we had a yoke of oxen, one of which spoiled at our stile before our door with blows up on the back and side so bruised that he was altogether unserviceable; about a fortnight or three weeks after the former we had a cow spoiled, her back broke and two*

of her ribs; nextly, I had a heifer in my barnyard, my earmark of which was cut out and other earmarks set on; nextly, I had a sow that had young pigs earmarked (in the sty) after the same manner; nextly, I had a cow at the side of my yard, her jawbone broke, and one of her hooves, and a hole bored in her side; nextly, I had a three year old heifer in the meadow stuck with a knife or some weapon and wounded to death;

Nextly, I had a cow in the street wounded in the bag, as she stood before my door, in the street; nextly, I had a sow went out into the woods, came home with ears luged [roughly pulled] *and one of her hind legs cut off; lastly, my corn in Mile Meadow much damnified with horses, they being staked upon it; it was wheat; all which injuries as they do savor of envy, so I hope they will be looked upon by this honored court, according to their nature, and judged according to their demerit, that so your poor suppliant may find some redress who is bold to subscribe.*[212]

Katherine was acquitted of the witchcraft charges in October 1668. However, the townsfolk's resentment of Katherine grew worse during that winter. The Court of Assizes indicted Katherine again on May 25, 1669, and she once more pleaded not guilty.[213] The complexities of the Katherine Harrison case greatly troubled the Court of Assizes magistrates, and they decided to postpone the trial until the next meeting. After all, Katherine's self-proclaimed fortune-telling abilities were explicitly stated, from witness testimonies and Katherine, to have been learned from the teachings of the English astrologer William Lilly and not from the devil. The ministers and magistrates of the court were learned men and also had an interest in these subjects, but they wouldn't consider themselves to be diabolical. For example, Governor John Winthrop, who presided over Katherine's trial, was an alchemist with an interest in natural magic as an extension of his studies in natural philosophy.[214] So, the magistrates had to find a compromise to appease the townsfolk of Wethersfield, while also not compromising their own intellectual curiosities.[215] The magistrates were thereby pressured to examine the particulars of Katherine's case in more detail. The Katherine Harrison case is a clear example of the entanglement of law and theology that defined this period. The magistrates, as sympathetic and pious as they were, were finally forced to legally define the descriptions and conditions of diabolical witchcraft. These definitions would set a precedent for how all future cases would be tried.

In May 1669, following Katherine's second indictment, the magistrates deferred to a group of Hartford ministers, likely led by Gershom Bulkely,[216] to address several issues regarding this case. Four main questions were asked of the ministers:

(1) Whether a plurality of witnesses be necessary, legally, to evidence one and the same individual fact

(2) Whether the preternatural apparition of a person, legally proved, be a demonstration of familiarity with the Devil

(3) Whether a vicious person's foretelling some future event, or revealing of a secret, be a demonstration of familiarity with the Devil

(4) Whether harm inflicted by a person's specter or apparition, if legally proven, was proof of diabolism[217]

The ministers worked to answer these questions over the next five months. They were not prepared with the answers when the Court of Assizes reconvened on October 12, 1669. The jury found Katherine guilty of the indictment, ordered to pay all of her legal fees and ultimately be put to death.[218] Fortunately, the ministers delivered their analysis and responses to the questions on October 20, 1669. The magistrates, after receiving the long rebuttal of Katherine Harrison, who offered to submit herself to the "water test" and reading the ministers' document, moved to reconvene in a "special session" the following May to reexamine Katherine's case. The ministers' responses to the magistrates questions reads as follows:

(1) Question: "Whether a plurality of witnesses be necessary, legally, to evidence one and the same individual fact"

(1) Response: "A plurality of witnesses" are necessary to demonstrate evidence of an individual event in question. The ministers justified this by referring to the biblical verse John 8:17, that states, "It is also written in your law, that the testimony of two men is true."

The ministers had faith that God would intervene and protect the righteous and pious against false testimony and further justified their decision by quoting Matthew 26:59–60 that states, "Now the chief priests, and elders, and all the council, sought false witness against Jesus, to put him to death; But found none: yea, though many false witnesses came, yet found they none. At the last came two false witnesses."[219] *(King James Version)*

(2) Question: "Whether the preternatural apparition of a person, legally proved, be a demonstration of familiarity with the Devil"

(2) Response: "*We answer that it is not the pleasure of the most high, to suffer the wicked one to make, an undistinguishable representation, of any innocent person in a way of doing mischief, before a plurality of witnesses.*" They follow up by stating that, practically, if the Devil could take the shape of any innocent person, then anyone's testimony could be called into question and mayhem would reign.[220] However, both magistrates and ministers absolutely believed that the Devil could take on the shape of a specific person.[221] The challenge was to define this phenomenon legally in order to justify prosecution.[222]

(3) Question: "*Whether a vicious person's foretelling some future event, or revealing of a secret, be a demonstration of familiarity with the Devil*"

(3) Response: "*That those things, whether past, present, or to come, which are indeed secret, that is cannot be known by human skill in arts, or strength of reason arguing from the course of nature, nor are made known by divine revelation either mediate or immediate, nor by information from man, must needs be known (if at all) by information from the Devil: and hence the communication of such things, in way of divination (the person pretending the certain knowledge of them) seems to us, to argue familiarity with the Devil, inasmuch as such a person, doth thereby declare his receiving of the Devil's testimony, and yield the Devil's instrument to communicate the same to others.*"[223]

The Hartford minsters had lived through and overseen many witch trials and understood the hysteria caused by them, such as the witchcraft outbreak in Hartford in 1661. Gershom Bulkely and his fellow ministers approached this case and the aforementioned questions carefully to prevent another hysteria. However, the use of spectral evidence was a serious matter: on one hand, God would never allow the devil to take on the shape of an innocent person. On the other hand, God's all-knowing plan was impossible to interpret or decipher.[224] To address this, the ministers referred to their response concerning the plurality of witness testimony. Cases where a malefic apparition was reported to cause harm rarely produced two or more witnesses, and the ministers knew the difficulty of getting multiple witnesses to testify to the same supernatural event.[225] The fourth question, therefore, was answered in the belief that the Lord would not allow the devil to take on the shape of an innocent person.

Although Katherine was found guilty and sentenced to death, based on the ministers' responses to the theological problems outlined in the case, the magistrates found the punishment to be inappropriate and instead ordered Katherine to leave Wethersfield. The wording in the order implies that Katherine had already made the decision to leave.[226] Katherine decided to move to the town of Westchester, New York (present-day Westchester Square, Bronx). The town of Westchester was an established village and presumably far enough from the negative rumors that surrounded Katherine. One could imagine how Katherine traveled to New York by boat, or perhaps she followed the Connecticut River south until reaching the Long Island Sound, then traveled west along the coast until she came to Westchester, especially considering how the Connecticut River was used as a landscape feature to direct travel.[227] Katherine's sixteen-year-old daughter, Rebeckah, had married Josiah Hunt of Westchester, and it is likely Katherine stayed with this daughter on her arrival. Unfortunately, Katherine and her daughter (or perhaps her new son-in-law) had some disagreement over the late John Harrison's property, which young Rebeckah claimed was left to her. This disagreement may have led to the revival of witchcraft accusations against Katherine in this new town.[228] The complaints against her were leveled by Thomas Hunt Sr., Josiah's father. Regardless, news of her previous witchcraft accusations and the guilty verdict surely would have made the settlers of Westchester uneasy with her arrival. Thomas Hunt Sr. was supported by the townsfolk of Westchester in a petition to the governor to remove her from their village and prevent her from wreaking havoc similar to the reports they heard from Wethersfield, Connecticut. Governor Lovelace first attempted to appease the villagers by ordering the removal of Katherine. His order reads as follows:

An order for Katherine Harrison to remove from Westchester.

Whereas complaint hath been made unto me by the inhabitants of Westchester against Katherine Harrison, late of Wethersfield in his majesty's colony of Connecticut, widow. That contrary to the consent and good liking of the town she would settle amongst them and she being reputed to be a person lying under the suspicion of witchcraft hath given some cause of apprehension to the inhabitants there, to the end there jealousies and fears as to this particular may be removed, I have thought fit to order and appoint that the Constable and Overseers of the Town of Westchester do

give warning to the said Katherine Harrison to remove out of their precincts in some short time after notice given and they are likewise to admonish her to return to the place of her former abode that they nor their neighbors may receive no further disturbance by her, given under my hand at Fort James in New York this 7th day of July, 1670
—Governor Francis Lovelace [229]

However, Katherine had been through a rough ordeal in Connecticut from which she emerged, undefeated, with her life. She knew the accusations, tribulations and whispers would not end until she took a stand and so she refused to leave her new refuge. After all, if she could not stay there, then where was she to go? She found temporary refuge with Captain Richard Panton, a resident of Westchester. It is unclear if she had formerly known Captain Panton, perhaps a colleague or associate of her late husband's merchant ventures, or just a good Samaritan she met on arrival. Regardless, another notice was sent to the governor of her refusal to vacate, to which the governor sent a follow-up order, summoning both Katherine and Captain Panton to appear before him immediately to answer for their disobedience. This order reads as follows:

An order for Katherine Harrison and Captain Richard Panton to appear at the fort before the Governor.

Whereas complaint has been made unto me by the inhabitants of Westchester against Katherine Harrison widow, that she does neglect to refuse or obey my late order concerning her removal out of the said town, these are to require you that you give notice unto the said Katherine Harrison as also unto Captain Richard Panton at whose house she resides, that they make their personal appearance before me in this place on Wednesday next being the 24th of this instant month, when those of the town that have ought to object against them do likewise attend, where I shall endeavor a composure of this difference between them.
Given under my hand at Fort James in New York on this 20th day of August 1670
—Governor Francis Lovelace [230]

Katherine Harrison and Captain Richard Panton traveled fourteen miles to Fort James to plead their case in front of the sympathetic Governor Lovelace. This meeting seems to have gone as well as they could have hoped. The next day, Governor Lovelace first ordered the constable of Westchester to create an inventory of Katherine's belongings as collateral for her good behavior within the New York jurisdiction. On the same day, he issued an order stating that she was permitted to remain in Westchester, that she had provided sufficient collateral for her good behavior in the colony and that he was skeptical that the complaints against her were legitimate. Two months later, he released her from any obligations and collateral for her good behavior and said she was free to travel and live anywhere in the colony. The successive orders reads as follows:

> *To the Constable of Westchester,*
> *A warrant to the Constable of Westchester to take an account of the goods of Katherine Harrison.*
>   *These are to require you to take an account of such goods as has lately been brought from out of his majesty's colony of Connecticut unto Katherine Harrison and having taken a note of the particulars that you return the same unto me for the doing whereof this shall be your warrant. Given under my hand at Fort James in New York this 25th day of August 1670*
> *—Governor Francis Lovelace*[231]

*

> *To the present constable of West Chester,*
>
> *An order concerning Katherine Harrison.*
> *Whereas several addresses have been made unto me by some of the inhabitants of Westchester on behalf of the rest desiring that Katherine Harrison late of Wethersfield in his majesty's colony of Connecticut widow at present residing in their town may be ordered to remove from thence and not permitted to stay within their jurisdiction upon an apprehension they have of her grounded upon some troubles she had lain under at Wethersfield upon suspicion of witchcraft, the reasons whereof do not clearly appear unto me, yet notwithstanding to give as much satisfaction as may be to the complainants who pretend their fears to be of public concern, I have not thought fit absolutely to determine the matter at present but do suspend it until the next General Court of Assizes, when there will be a full meeting of the council and justices of the peace to debate and conclude the same. In the meantime the said Katherine Harrison with her children may remain in the Town of Westchester where she now is without disturbance or molestation, she having given sufficient security for her civil carriage and good behavior.*

Given under my hand at Fort James in New York this 25th day of August in the 22nd year of his majesty's reign Anno Domini 1670
—*Governor Francis Lovelace* [232]

*

An 1670 Appeals, Actions, Presentments, ect., Entered for hearing and trial at the General Court of Assizes to be held in New York beginning on the first Wednesday of October 1670

Kathryn Harrison bound over to appear upon the complaint of the inhabitants of Westchester under suspicion of witchcraft.

In the case of Katherine Harrison, widow, who is bound to the good behavior upon complaint of some of the inhabitants of Westchester until the holding of this court, it is ordered, that in regard there is nothing appears against her deserving the continuance of that obligation she is to be released from it and have liberty to remain in the Town of Westchester where she now resides or anywhere else in the government during her pleasure.
—*Governor Francis Lovelace* [233]

Katherine could not escape the gossip and petty harassment in her new home and was pressured to depart from her residence in Westchester. Unfortunately, Katherine could not escape her reputation and presumed status as an outlaw and was continually harassed and identified as a presumably easy target for robbery. For example, Katherine entrusted some of her papers to Francis (or Robert) Yates for safekeeping. Yates refused to hand them back over, claiming he had a lien on the items. So, Katherine filed a complaint to the governor. The governor, in turn, ordered the constables and overseers to help Katherine retrieve all of her possessions from Yates and asserted that if Yates or anyone had "pretenses of debt…or damage…that they should follow the course of the law…and that no person is allowed to be the judge of his own cause." [234] Following this incident, Thomas Hunt, the chief complainant of her presence in Westchester, and her daughter's father-in-law, sued her for her daughter's marriage portion. Katherine denied ever making claims to "pay any sum of money to her daughter in marriage to her husband." The constable of Westchester seized her property that was in the town and also her property aboard the boat of Theophilus Ellsworth, who was hired to transport her out of Westchester. Once more, she filed a complaint with the governor, who, on May 19, 1671, ordered the release of her property from the town of Westchester but also ordered Katherine to show up at the next Court of Assizes held at Jamaica, New York.[235]

Some evidence may indicate she actually moved farther east, onto Long Island. For example, the Court of Assizes issued a warrant to "any of the constables or other officers upon Long Island" to help her recover certain missing "goods."[236] This was certainly an effort of the governor to protect Katherine from any other attacks on her property by those who might see her as an easy target. Another theory places Katherine in the Dividend community (present-day Rocky Hill, Connecticut) outside of Wethersfield.[237] Further, there is a possibility that more witchcraft accusations were filed against her during the brief regain of New York by the Dutch, though these records no longer exist.[238] Whatever the case may be, this is the last we hear of Katherine Harrison in the pages of history.

10

MAES CORNELIS VAN BLOEMENDAAL / VAN BUREN

Maes Cornelis Van Bloemendaal (born Van Buren),[239] most often referred to only as Maes (or Maas) Cornelis was a Dutch settler born in Rensselaerswijck, New Netherland (present-day Albany, New York), sometime around 1643.[240] While the specific charge of witchcraft is not mentioned in his case, he was nevertheless accused of making an allegiance with the devil, a crime for which many women accused of witchcraft were executed in the early modern era. There is no specific mention of harm stemming from his allegiance with the devil, and quite honestly, his account just barely qualifies him for entry into this section. However, being accused of abandoning God and turning to the devil was a serious accusation in this period and connects pretty tightly to the root injustice of all bewitchment cases, namely, the diabolical nature of an accused individual forming a compact with the "great enemy of mankind," Satan. Therefore, Maes Cornelis's account is included and his story told.

Maes was the third son of Cornelis Maessen Van Buren, an early settler of New Netherland. At some point during his life, Maes decided to change his surname from Van Buren to Van Bloemendaal (Bloomingdale). Oddly, Maes was the only one of his siblings to make this moniker change. It is suspected that Maes named his farm and estate Bloemendaal, and since surnames were often a reference to a familial home, Maes had the foresight to start his own lineage in the so-called New World.[241]

Maes was accused of turning to the devil while he was in his late thirties. Fortunately for Maes, no one paid any mind to his accuser, Jan van Loon.

First Church in Albany. *Photograph by author.*

Instead, Jan van Loon found himself at the center of a slander accusation by the town sheriff Richard Pretty, who overheard the accusation. The following investigation and trial are found in the Court Minutes of Albany 1680–1685[242] and read as follows:

> *Richard Pretty, sheriff, plaintiff, against Jan van Loon, defendant.*
>
> *The plaintiff, ex officio, charges the defendant in writing with having on the 27th of December last, while at the house of Albert Rykman, strongly denounced and slandered the person of Maes Cornelise in the presence of several witnesses, because, having heretofore been a Papist, he had on the 22nd of the said month made his confession of faith of the Reformed religion before the consistory and hence been accepted as a member of the church, saying that Maes Cornelise was a renegade and from God had turned to the devil, all of which the plaintiff undertakes to prove. And whereas such unheard of and Godless blasphemy and slanderous language against the Protestant religion, which is supported and maintained by express command of his Majesty, cannot be tolerated, he requests the court, as Christian judges and fosterers of God's church and community, first, to order the defendant humbly to pray God and the Reformed congregation of this town, or those who represent the same, for forgiveness for his slanderous language,*

and [secondly] *to condemn him to such corporal punishment as their honors shall see fit and to the payment of a fine of fl.800 in seawan, one-third for the benefit of the poor of the Reformed church here and the other two-thirds for the benefit of the officer, cum expensis, requesting further that he may be bound over for his good behavior during the period of two years, as an example to others.*

Jan van Loon totally denies that he ever spoke such words; yes, says [that] *he never thought and did not know that the sheriff would bring such action against him, and requests time to make answer.*

He is answered that he was summoned by warrant about the matter and that he could have found the plaintiff's declaration at the secretary's office three days before the session of the court, to which he replied that he did not know anything about it.

The testimony continues:

Eghbert Teunise, being sworn, says that on the 27th of December last he came to the house of Albert Rykman, where Jan van Loon and Jan Gow were sitting and that he had some conversation with Jan van Loon about the preaching of Dom. Bernardus, minister of the church of the Augsburg Confession. Eghbert being asked what he thought of it, he said that he spoke a little loud; that his text was good, but that in his opinion he was a little prolix and furthermore, that he did not believe what he preached, namely, that Mary the Virgin, or the Virgin Mary, died a virgin, unless he could prove it by the Bible. Conversing further, Jan van Loon spoke to Jan Gow and [a]*bout Maes Cornelis, saying that Maes Cornelis was like a renegade in Turkey; that he had forsaken his God and embraced the devil. And further he knows not.*

Reynier Quackeboss, being sworn, declare that he was also present there and that he heard Jan Gow having some conversation with Jan van Loon about H. Rutgers, namely, that he was lost in the woods and that wolves had come near him, but that he had finally found the right path, whereupon Jan van Loon said: "What do I care about Maes Cornelise? He is like a renegade in Turkey; he has forsaken God and embraced the devil."

Jan Cornelise Vyselar, alias Jan Gow, being sworn, declares that he heard Albert and Jan van Loon converse about religion at the said time and that he, the deponent, had some further discussion with Jan van Loon about H. Rutgers, who was lost in the woods, and how afraid he had been when the wolves came near home, but that he had struck the right path again, to which Jan van Loon replied: "Maes Cornelis also lost his way; he is like a renegade in Turkey; he has forsaken God and embraced the devil."

Andries Albertse Bradt, being sworn, says that there was some dispute, but he paid no attention to it and knows nothing about the matter.

Robert Sanders, being sworn, says that the next day he spoke to Jan van Loon and advised him to settle the dispute, to which Jan van Loon replied: "What have I done? I have said nothing wrong. If I said anything, I will prove it."

Jan van Loon for his further exculpation says that he had some conversation with Eghbert Teunise about Dom. Bernardus and that Eghbert said that he had preached falsely and what he could not prove. Thereupon, Nell, the wife of Albert, began to speak of Maes and said: "Maes will convert you yet." To which he replied: "Whoever has the true faith and forsakes it, forsakes God and goes to the devil." And he says that he did not say such words as the witnesses testify.

The defendant requests that the wife of Albert Rykman may be summoned and examined, as she was present from the beginning.

Nell, the wife of Albert Rykman, being sworn, says that she does not know how the matter started, but that she heard Jan van Loon say: "What is Maes now? He is a renegade, who has forsaken God and sworn allegiance to the devil." Whereupon Nell said: "I call upon you to be my witness" and being much perturbed, added: "I shall inform Maes of it."

The Jury bring in their verdict that the defendant is guilty of blasphemy.

The honorable court, finding that the defendant by the jury is declared guilty of blasphemy, according to the sworn testimony in the matter, have after mature deliberation, unanimously resolved and decided to refer the judgment of such a crime to the next court of Assize, who will render sentence in the matter, and to have the delinquent taken immediately into custody, until he gives sufficient bail in the sum of £500 sterling at the secretary's office here for his appearance there, the plaintiff being ordered to prosecute the case against him there and the defendant to be mean-while of good behavior.

His mittimus

Whereas Mr. Jan van Loon by a decision of the court has this day been ordered to be taken into custody until he give security in the sum of £500 at the secretary's office here for his appearance before the next Court of Assizes to defend himself against the charges brought against him by the sheriff, to *wit, that on the 27th of December last, at the house of Albert Rykman, he spoke in a slanderous and blasphemous way about the Reformed religion, as appears from the proceedings in the matter; you are hereby ordered in his Majesty's name to take the person of the said Jan van Loon into custody and to guard him well until he shall have given security in the sum of £500 sterling for his appearance as above. For doing which this will be your sufficient warrant.* Actum *in Albany, as the session of their honors, January 3, 1681/2.*[243]

Jan van Loon, accuser, was a French papist from Liège, Belgium, and worked as a blacksmith in the Dutch colony.[244] His house[245] still stands as a historical site along the Hudson River in Athens, New York. It is unclear if Maes and Jan ever resolved their differences. We do know that on April 7, 1685, Jan van Loon and Maes served together on a jury, deliberating on a local dispute.[246] While this mutual duty may not be very insightful, another later trial once more included both Jan and Cornelis. In this trial, Jan van Loon claimed he was denied his full payment for a bartering transaction with Gerrit Lambertse. Jan asked the court to reconvene the following day so that he might gather evidence of the transaction and the failure of Gerrit to deliver the complete payment. However, it took Gerrit longer than a day to gather his own evidence, so he sent Maes Cornelis to relay a message to the court. Maes requested that the court be prolonged another day so that Gerrit could represent himself and he "further alleges that the defendant regrets that he signed such bond, saying that he was talked into it."[247] Nevertheless, the court ordered Gerrit to pay Jan eighty guilders in beaver furs. It is unclear if this favor for Gerrit was one of solidarity or simply responsibility. Did Maes help the defendant, Gerrit Lambertse, in his case because of persisting resentment toward the plaintiff, Jan van Loon? We may never know.

Overall, It's difficult to identify any conclusive accounts of witchcraft fear and accusations within Dutch communities, that is, Dutch settlers accusing other Dutch settlers. There are certain ingredients found in witchcraft accusations, and if we are to examine the recipe of other local historical accounts then we find no clear-cut example in Dutch communities. However, this is certainly not to say the belief in witches did not exist in these communities at all—just that authorities were cautious to lend these accusations any merit. For the historian, the claim that Dutch settlers entertained ideas of witches and harmful spiritual forces may seem peculiar. After all, prolific Dutch thinkers who were raised in old New Netherland like

Jan Van Loon House. Athens, New York. *Google Earth.*

Jacob Melyn wrote of their skepticism that humans could sign pacts with the devil and subsequently wreak havoc on their neighbors, while also criticizing the events at Salem in 1692.[248] Historian George Lincoln Burr credits Dutch intellectuals like Johann Weyer, Balthazar Bekker and Arminian Grevius with weighty contributions toward changing Dutch sentiments on the possibility of witchcraft.[249] However, an archaeological examination of Dutch artifacts in domestic New Netherland sites offers a peek into early Dutch American beliefs. Many homesteads of Dutch American settlers contained a vast array of apotropaic items and symbols intended to protect the dwellers from spiritual attacks by malevolent forces.[250] In fact, one example of these protective symbols and items can be observed at the homestead of Albertus van Loon, in Athens, New York.[251] Albertus is the son of Jan van Loon, the chief accuser of Maes Cornelis. Admittedly, the inclusion of Maes in this book as an "accused witch" is not truly set on any strong foundation. After all, his account struggles to fit the "recipe" for a witchcraft accusation as seen in other accounts. Maes was accused of being a renegade from God and turning to the devil, but there is no one really harmed and no spectral evidence submitted to support the accusation for the crime.

11

HANNAH HORTON HILDRETH BOWER TRAVALLY (TREVALLE)

Goody Garlick wasn't the only European person accused of witchcraft in the Hamptons, an area once thought sobered of hysteria in 1658. In fact, the second woman accused of witchcraft was Hannah (Horton Hildreth Bower) Travally and occurred only twenty-five years later in 1683. Very little is written about Hannah's life, but such is the case for women in the historical record, which has largely favored the lives and accomplishments of men over those of women. During the seventeenth century, settler women only appear in the historical record when mentioned in marriages or wills, and tracing them through time often relies on mentions of their husbands within court documents.

What we do know is that Hannah was the daughter and fourth child of Barnabas Horton and born sometime in the early 1630s in Leicestershire, Warwickshire, England.[252] Her father, Barnabas, is an interesting character in his own right: he started out as a less-than-prosperous baker in England and became an influential landowner on Long Island, thus beginning the Horton family in the Americas.[253] Hannah appears numerous times throughout court records, as she remarried three times and gave birth to at least eight children.[254] She is mentioned in the wills of her father and three husbands. Her first marriage was to Thomas Hildreth, a landowner in Southampton, New York, and the couple had four children.[255] Although Thomas spent a lot of time doing business in Southold, Thomas and Hannah Hildreth lived together in an area of Southampton known as Flying Point on the western banks of Mecox Bay. Thomas left this home

A map of Flying Point Area, Water Mill, Southampton, New York. *Google Earth*.

to his second-eldest son, Joseph, in his will when he passed away around 1657; Hannah was likely in her late twenties.[256]

After the passing of her husband Thomas, Hannah married Jonas Bower, who was a weaver in Southampton, and with Jonas, she had four more children.[257] Hannah likely moved into Jonas's home on Seabonac Neck, an area of land between Cold Spring Pond and Bullhead Bay, until he died in 1671 at around forty years old.[258] Jonas Bower, similar to Thomas Hildreth, states in his will that Hannah was to receive temporary ownership of the house until his son Jonah (Jr.) came of age.[259] This area of land is now the Seabonack Golf Club; the neighborhoods of the seventeenth century are long gone, and the cost of membership in this exclusive club is over half a million dollars.

By now, she had experienced the death of two spouses, and we can only imagine how that must have affected her. What trauma does that kind of loss entail, and what systems of support did she have available in bereavement? Hannah ultimately remarried once more, to Thomas Travally (or Trevalle), who arrived in 1666 and worked as a cooper[260] in Southampton.[261] Thomas and Hannah married after 1671 following the passing of her second husband, Jonas. Unfortunately, her father, Barnabas Horton, passed away in 1681, during Hannah's third marriage, and in his will left her ten sheep.[262]

Two years later, a neighbor, Edward Lacy, accused Hannah of witchcraft. Hannah's husband, Thomas, defended his wife from the accusations of Lacy, who claimed she set his corn on fire and sat on his house at night.

The gate to the historic Seabonac Neck area, now a golf course. *Photograph by author.*

He also claimed he had been "haggridden" (sleep paralysis/nightmares) by her bewitchment for three nights. By this time, Hannah was in her fifties, a common age for women to be accused of witchcraft. The passing of two previous husbands, her father and potentially infant children may have hardened Hannah in life. We do not know if it was Hannah or her husband, Thomas, who aggravated Edward Lacy to prompt him in his accusation, but Lacy had a difficult time arousing the settlers of Southampton against Hannah. After all, who was Edward Lacy but a passerby with no permanent stake in Southampton, while Hannah was a lifelong resident with ties to not only the Horton family but also the Hildreths and the Bowers. The court ultimately ruled in favor of the Travally family and ordered Lacy to pay a fine of three shillings and six pence.[263] This account appears in Howell's history of Southampton, although Howell doesn't provide a source or further information for this trial. Edward Lacy is not found in the historical record of Southampton after this event and possibly moved out of town. Hannah's third husband, Thomas, died four years later in 1687/8 at the age of forty-six.[264] Hannah lived to nearly seventy years old.

12

GOODWIFE MILLER

Goodwife Miller was a woman from Fairfield, Connecticut, who was accused of witchcraft in 1692 by a servant girl, Katherine (Kate) Branch of Stamford, who was likely attempting to imitate the Salem Witch Trials occurring nearly one hundred miles away in the neighboring Massachusetts Bay Colony.[265] Unfortunately, we do not know her given name and are left with only the moniker Goodwife Miller along with primary source mentions of familial relationships that are obscure and unresolved. Goodwife Miller's story intersects with New York history, as she ultimately fled from her home in Connecticut after Kate's accusation and decamped to Bedford, Westchester County, New York. Goody Miller's life is interesting in that, as with many other accounts in this book, there is really not much known about her life. She briefly pops into the written historical record in 1692 and just as easily disappears after 1697. This small window of time is all that we know of her life and therefore demands quite a bit of our attention. A more in-depth account of this case can be found in Richard Godbeer's *Escaping Salem: The Other Witch Hunt of 1692* (2005).

Goodwife Miller's arrival in the historical record begins in April 1692 after the strange behavior of a servant girl named Katherine Branch. Being a servant was not uncommon and did not necessarily imply poverty. In fact, many children were sent away from their homes to live with neighbors or extended family in order to learn responsibility, skills or trades, occasionally if parents felt they had spoiled their children a bit too

Arresting a witch, by Howard Pyle (1853–1911). *The New York Public Library Digital Collections.*

much and needed to teach them some discipline and humility.[266] This form of servitude was not necessarily a duty for life, and many children would reach adulthood, marry and start families of their own. It's easy to imagine that Kate Branch, like most young girls of her time, dreamed of marrying a well-to-do young man, having a home and a family and living a comfortable life. Unfortunately, Kate's situation was bit different, as she was a penniless orphan under the charge of Daniel and Abigail Wescot. With no parents or inheritance for a dowry, Kate's prospects of marrying into a good family were slim (but certainly not impossible).[267]

By April 1692, the Salem Witch Trials had persisted for nearly four months and news of the witch endemic had spread through the colonies. Nearly one hundred miles away sat Daniel and Abigail Wescot's home in Stamford, Connecticut, where they lived with their daughters and servant Kate Branch.[268] One of their daughters, Joanna, had been afflicted by "strange pains and frights" years earlier, having claimed that creatures entered her room and ran around to different hiding places, causing her pain.[269] Although her father, Daniel, suspected witchcraft, Joanna was sent to live at a friend's house for a few months and the issue was resolved. Witchcraft was a real malady for New England settlers, and surely, since Joanna had recovered, the Wescots were happy to push the idea of witchcraft from their minds and move on to avoid any further possible occult complications. In a manner of speaking, occult complications would soon find them.

In April 1692, Abigail Wescot instructed Kate to collect herbs for the family and became irritated when Kate returned empty-handed. Kate returned, having not collected any herbs, and began rolling on the floor in agony from chest pain. Abigail was suspicious of Kate's performance from the onset.[270] Daniel Wescot was far more sensitive than his wife, and Abigail feared her husband's witchcraft trauma from their daughter Joanna's event would once again afflict and excite Daniel's weak constitution. In later testimonies, Abigail's niece Lydia Penoyer was recorded as having said:

She [Lydia Penoyer] *said that she heard her aunt Abigail Wescot say that her servant girl Katherine Branch was such a lying girl that not anybody could believe one word what she said and* [also] *says that she heard her aunt Abigail Wescot say that she did not believe that Mercy nor Goody Miller nor Hannah nor any of these women whom she had appeached was any more witches than she was and that her husband would believe Katherine before he would believe Mr. Bishop or Lieutenant Bell or herself.*[271]

The Wescots decided to call for the town's healer, Sarah Bates. Sarah Bates was an impressive character herself, as she had a solid reputation for her medical skills.[272] Sarah, equipped with traditional and practical knowledge of healthcare and herbs could identify symptoms, diagnose maladies and develop treatment plans despite having no known formal training, apprenticeship or university degree. Sarah had some ideas about what kind of natural causes were afflicting Kate. For example, Kate had experienced fainting and chest pains; she was "seized with a pinching and pricking at her breast."[273] Sarah also knew Kate's late mother had a history of the falling sickness (now known as epilepsy).[274] Sarah instructed the Wescot family to burn feathers under Kate's nose, which Sarah had found to be effective in treating fainting. While this treatment worked at first, Kate's condition ultimately worsened. Sarah was called for again, as Kate had seemingly fallen into a coma.

The Wescots and Sarah gathered around the unconscious body of Kate Branch as they discussed treatment plans and what could be the cause of this condition. Abigail Wescot and Sarah approached this issue logically to identify a natural cause and subsequent remedy. It was possible there was an imbalance of Kate's humors. During this period of history, all sickness was traditionally believed to be caused by a fluid imbalance in the body. The four bodily fluids (or humors) were blood, phlegm, choler and melancholy, and sickness could be remedied by restoring the equilibrium of one or more of these fluids. Mrs. Wescot suggested bloodletting in an attempt to balance the four humors. Sarah saw the logic but cautioned that bloodletting a comatose patient was risky since the patient was so close to death. Nevertheless, Mrs. Wescot insisted on bloodletting. As Sarah was about to prick Kate with a pin, all of Kate's symptoms suddenly vanished, and she exclaimed, "I'll not be blooded!"[275] Sarah asked, "Why not?" and Kate replied, "Because it will hurt!" Mrs. Wescott assured Kate that it would be only a quick, minor pain, and they proceeded to prick Kate's foot and let blood. The procedure went well, and Kate rested in bed. After a moment, Kate began to belt out a bloodcurdling scream while one of the Wescot daughters cried out, "Mother!," to which Mrs. Wescot replied, "She is bewitched!"[276] To the Wescots' confusion, Kate began to laugh hysterically into her pillow. Was this a symptom of bewitchment, or was Kate amused by her own theatrical performance?[277] Kate's delusions worsened in the following days, and soon her imagination created scenes of witchcraft that began to relate specific individual accusations.

Kate began to see a black cat that "invited her to go away to a place where there were fine things and fine people," images of feast spreads with a variety of meats.[278] The more Daniel Wescot bought into these fantasies, the more elaborate they became. Now Kate claimed to see a total of ten cats eating at a table and that she was no longer invited to dine with them. In fact, the cats threatened to kill her since she told Daniel Wescot of them. She stated that a cat was approaching her with a dead rat clutched in its mouth, ready to fling the carcass at Kate.[279] These stories grew more elaborate over time, with the cats transforming into women, yet to be identified.

Daniel Wescot must have felt at least a little foolish for entertaining these fantasies. He knew that his neighbors suspected that Kate was faking her symptoms, and so he invited them to help observe and comfort her. Daniel must have so desperately wanted confirmation of his supernatural suspicions that he presumably invited his more credulous neighbors. Daniel's friends David Selleck and Abraham Finch agreed to help Daniel observe Kate and protect her from bewitchment the best they could. Daniel had to leave for a business trip to Hartford and needed help with caring for Kate in this condition.[280] This task was surely a mark of bravery for David and Abraham, who were already frightened by the thought of bewitchment far before they arrived at the Wescot home. The pair arrived, dramatically, at night and were greeted with the polite formalities of conversation and cider fireside. One can only imagine their anxiety during that small talk as they awaited the inevitable tour upstairs to where they would stand guard as a bewitched servant girl lay sleeping—or waiting. As the night progressed, Mrs. Wescot led the way to Kate's room, where she was sound asleep. Someone needed to sit close to Kate to restrain her in the event of bewitched convulsions during the night. David agreed to stand first watch, sitting on a bed inches away from Kate, while Abraham occupied a different corner of the room.[281] Suddenly, a scream came from the adjoining room. David jumped and examined Kate, but she was still fast asleep. He looked at Abraham, who exited the room to investigate. Abraham returned and reported that one of the Wescot daughters had a nightmare and was being tended to by Mrs. Wescot. It was a good time as any to be relieved, and Abraham took David's seat while David exited the room with a lantern and paced the floor in the adjoining room with anxiety. Suddenly there came another scream—and his time from Kate's room. David rushed back in to find "Abraham sitting up on the bed deathly pale and Kate lying at his feet."[282] Abraham told David that after Kate had screamed, he witnessed "a ball of fire as big as my two hands pass across the room to the hearth and then it disappeared."[283] But what strange phenomena, fear-induced hallucination or elaborate sleight of hand could have produced this effect? Abraham was dumbfounded and disturbed. It was David's turn to stand watch.

Abraham relocated to a nearby chest to sit and collect himself while David took to the bed beside Kate. David lay down, waiting out his shift, when he suddenly he felt a sharp prick in his side. He called out to Abraham in pain and exclaimed, "She pricked me!" Kate quickly replied, "No I didn't….It was Goody Crump." However, no one had ever heard of anyone named Goody Crump. Kate spoke into the ether and said, "Give me that thing [which] you pricked Mr. Selleck with." With a sleight of hand, Kate closed her empty hand and then produced a pin to hand to Abraham.[284] The two men were convinced: Kate was bewitched. Further, Kate had yet to identify who Goody Crump was.

Linda Maestra! (Pretty Teacher!) (1799) by Francisco José de Goya y Lucientes. *The New York Public Library Digital Collections.*

In the following nights, different neighbors took over in shifts to watch Kate and help the Wescot family in caring for their servant. One night, Ebenezer Bishop was observing Kate, when she complained of being pinched by the apparition of Goody Clawson.[285] During another night, Samuel Holly reported that he watched Kate's breasts inflate like bladders and collapse into her body, with an unnatural rattling sound coming from her throat.[286] It seemed the more performances she pulled off in front of Daniel Wescot's neighbors, the more attention and amusement she received. Daniel's supernatural beliefs were also reaffirmed before each neighbor who would stand a shift watching Kate and leave with their own unique story to share with the others afterward. Still, others in the town were not convinced that this all wasn't some elaborate performance by Kate. This skepticism only fueled Daniel's belief in Kate's bewitchment. In fact, it needed to reinforce Daniel's beliefs, since if Kate made this all up then Daniel would have been made to look incredibly foolish being tricked by his own servant girl. This embarrassment would be unacceptable. Daniel was so eager to deny any fabrication of Kate's unnatural bewitchment that he told neighbors, "I'll venture both my cows against a calf that she'll do a trick tomorrow morning that nobody else can."[287] His defensiveness and pride were pushing him to make such claims that ultimately implicated him. Neighbor Abigail Cross challenged this statement, "Can you make her do it when you want?" to which he replied, "Yes…when I want, I can make her do it."[288] Over time, several neighbors observed Kate's strange and suspicious behavior. In some instances, right when observers thought they outwitted Kate and caught her in fabricated performance, some unexplainable strange event occurred that reaffirmed unnatural bewitchment.

But who was her alleged tormenter? Who was Goody Crump? It wasn't long before Kate began to identify multiple people as her alleged tormenters, certain specific women in the community. Among the several women named during Kate's fits, she identified Goody Crump not by her recognized Christian name but by her appearance: "a short and lame old woman…hook backed…crump backed…[who] wore a homespun coat with a waistcoat underneath…[and a] black cap."[289] This description matched only one neighbor, Goodwife Miller. Now that Goodwife Miller had been named, Kate further related that she could see Goodwife Miller with a long witch's teat under her arm that she used to feed her black dog familiar. Kate cried out, "Goody Miller, hold up your arm higher that the black dog may suck you better. Now I'm sure you are a witch for you've got a long teat under your arm."[290]

Goody Miller heard about the accusations against her from Kate Branch and decided not to stick around while the town indulged the fantasies of a young girl. The most logical place to decamp to avoid prosecution was the nearby town of Bedford. Twelve years prior, in 1680, some families from Stamford decided to establish a new town roughly ten miles away. However, in 1683, the Connecticut/New York border was renegotiated, and Bedford was now part of New York's jurisdiction. This nearby village was a convenient and accessible location to escape to for a crippled elderly woman fleeing from her own community's hysteria. Goody Miller knew she would be protected since Bedford was out of Stamford's legal jurisdiction, but she also had two ace cards in her proverbial back pocket.

A white-faced witch meeting a black-faced witch with a great beast. Woodcut, 1720. *Wellcome Collection.*

Goody Miller had two brothers in Bedford: Abram Ambler, the town magistrate, and Joseph Theale, commander of the town's militia.[291] While they are referred to as her brothers in contemporary testimonies, the exact family relationship is unknown. It is also known that a John Miller Sr. was one of the original settlers of Bedford, although the relationship to Goody Miller of this account is also unknown.[292] Under the protection of such respectable and influential brothers, Goody Miller was well protected. Nevertheless, Daniel Wescot was not one to be made a fool of and personally pursued Goody Miller to Bedford to demand justice for crimes afflicted on his servant. Daniel demanded that they consign Miller over to him so that she could be prosecuted in Stamford. Judge John Pell of Westchester complied with Daniel Wescot's demand and agreed to hand Miller over to Connecticut authorities.[293] However, before Judge Pell could issue the order, he promptly rescinded his decision after a visit from a

"There is a flock of yellow birds around her head," Scene from the Salem Witch Trials, by Howard Pyle (1853–1911). *The New York Public Library Digital Collections.*

certain Bedford town magistrate along with the commander of the Bedford militia, Goodwife Miller's two brothers.[294] Goody Miller was staying put, and in comfort, for the time being.

Meanwhile, mayhem was ensuing back in Stamford. Kate Branch had accused not only Miller but also five other women: Elizabeth Clawson, Mercy Disborough, Mary Staples, Mary Harvey and Hannah Harvey.[295] These women were accused of a serious crime and needed to be brought to justice. However, the logistics of organizing a trial at Hartford, the seat of Connecticut Colony's colonial government, would be a daunting and problematic endeavor. Connecticut authorities decided to set up a temporary satellite court, a Court of Oyer and Terminer, so that the trial could take place in Stamford, thus requiring the Connecticut Colony governor, deputy governor and several magistrates to try the case in Stamford, rather than have all defendants and witnesses travel sixty-five miles to Hartford. This approach was set forth by the neighboring Massachusetts Bay Colony, which established its own temporary Oyer and Terminer Court in Salem during its contemporary witch trials.[296]

Goodwife Miller was smart to escape the excitement and hysteria unfolding in her town, especially since Stamford was divided over whether Kate's accusations were authentic or not. The midwife Sarah Bates was one of seventy-six townsfolk who were skeptical of the authenticity of Kate Branch's accusations and joined together to sign a petition in support of the accused women.[297] Still, the escape of Goody Miller greatly troubled the magistrates, particularly Stamford magistrate Jonathan Selleck, who had been following the development of these incidents from the start and truly believed Goody Miller to be evil.[298] A correspondence from Jonathan Selleck to colony official Nathan Gold indicates that Jonathan Selleck tried to use his political pull with Caleb Heathcote, commander of the Westchester militia and close friends with the New York governor, to foster the release of Miller to Connecticut authorities so that she could be brought to justice. This correspondence reads as follows:

Honored Sir. Due respects promised; Is to acquaint you that yesterday Sergeant Westcott brought his maid Kate down to my house to be examined; and I took her relation concerning how she had been afflicted of late which is too long to relate....But [I] *refer you to the bearer my son John Selleck who was a spectator with several more at the time—the poor girl was forced to stay all night and as yet not come to her senses; but when she is I shall examine her about what she discoursed in her fits; said Kate said also in her fits last night that there was a creature she saw among them with a great head and wings all black: and Kate asked the girl she called Hannah saying is that your father: I believe it is. Sir what may be in the matter the Lord knows; Mr. Pell and Justice Theale* [Goody Miller's brother] *would not do anything toward examining Goody Miller when they met at Bedford and the girl carried there by her master to the intent she might see if she knew Goody Miller from among other women but nothing was done; and the true reason I know not but think that Mr. Pell was discouraged by the woman's two brothers Mr. Theale and Mr. Ambler who was there; then Daniel Wescott desired Mr. Pell to order Goody Miller to be sent down hither; at first he said he would do it but advising with her brothers would not do it but said he would advise with the Attorney General Mr. Graham; but Abraham Ambler told Daniel Wescott he knew what would become of her is she was sent down to us here; he not being willing to it.*

Sir I have here enclosed sent [Peter Chafee's letter] *from Bedford which says that the Attorney General was not willing to encourage the proceedings against Goodwife Miller; but I am of the mind that if the authority here would send to the governor of New York for to order Goody Miller to be sent down to us that he would do it; and if any such thing be sent and a message on purpose I will write* [to] *improve my interest in Colonel Heathcote who hath the greatest interests in the present governor of any man in New York; for 'tis great pity she cannot be had; for I fear that all the persons the girl names are naught; and I desire the Lord to make discovery of them; which with mine and wife's best respects to yourself and kind sister and love to all our cousins I take leave and am assertedly your most affectionate brother Jonathan Selleck senior, Stanford, June 29, 1692 to the Honored Major Nathan Gold; Assistant present in Fairfield.*[299]

Jonathan Selleck's attempt to butter up Colonel Heathcote, whatever lickspittle words that were sent, went unheeded, and no known actions were taken by New York authorities. This was certainly a reflection of the contentious politics between New York and Connecticut at the time. The

The Bedford Historical Society adjacent to the Town of Bedford Old Burying Ground. Bedford, New York. *Photograph by author.*

Town of Bedford Old Burying Ground. Bedford, New York. *Photograph by author.*

failed rebellion of Jacob Leisler to claim New York, in years prior, was supported by Connecticut authorities, who provided Leisler with militiamen. The current colonial New York administration was greatly anti-Leislerian and would have staunchly rejected any pleas for political favors from Leisler's former political allies in Connecticut.[300] Political contention between New York and the New England colonies persisted with the incoming governor Benjamin Fletcher. Governor Fletcher was well aware of the situation at hand and how his predecessors' pleas for help to the Massachusetts Bay Colony to help defend against the Leisler/Connecticut alliance went unanswered as well. It was safe to say that New York would not be doing any favors to the New England colonies anytime soon, and New York became a "safe haven" for fugitives escaping trial and punishment from Connecticut and Massachusetts authorities.[301]

The five other women accused in Stamford were ultimately all acquitted, and it is unclear what became of Goodwife Miller. She fades out of history, like so many others, as quickly as she entered. If she remained with her brothers, then it is possible she was buried in the Old Burying Ground next to the Bedford Historical Society. Daniel Wescot and his family retained their respectability after the witchcraft excitement dissipated. Further, Daniel was reelected as a representative but ultimately moved his family to Cohansey, New Jersey, along with other migrants from Fairfield County, Connecticut.[302] It is unclear what happened to Katherine Branch, as she too fades from history.

13

THE SALEM REFUGEES

Between the years 1692 and 1693, the settlers of New England succumbed to their darkest fears of witchcraft, and so began the highest recorded volume of accusations and executions of suspected witches in American history. This period is notoriously known as the Salem Witch Trials and resulted in over one hundred people accused, with many being imprisoned or financially devastated and nineteen people[303] and two dogs publicly executed; one person was tortured to death and five people died in prison awaiting trial. However, a few were able to flee their hostile homes and escape accusation by seeking asylum in New York. Those witchcraft fugitives who were able to flee were some of the wealthier families that were accused, wealthy enough to afford a hasty escape out of the colony, no easy endeavor. During these years, three people accused in Salem are recorded temporarily living in New York until the mass hysteria settled in their hometowns. These accused individuals included Mary and Philip English and Elizabeth Cary with the support of her husband Nathaniel. Some records indicate that John Alden may have also fled to New York, but this idea remains controversial.[304] All of the aforementioned were sympathetically welcomed to New York by Governor Benjamin Fletcher, whose contentious relationship with the Connecticut and Massachusetts Bay Colonies created a kairos moment for refugees seeking protection. New York governor Benjamin Fletcher (in office 1692–97) was an odd character himself, having cavorted with pirates, tried to expand the borders of the New York colony and threatened to fistfight Governor William Phips of the Massachusetts Bay Colony. Fletcher was in office during the Golden Age of Piracy and gave way to pirate communities within his jurisdiction in return for a new stream of revenue into the colony as well as personal favors. Fletcher surely realized the vast amount of wealth pirates brought to the impoverished New York colony, some of which was used to directly pay off Fletcher to ignore their criminal activities.[305] Even Nicholas Bayard (Judith's husband from previous section) was a Benjamin Fletcher supporter.[306]

MARY ENGLISH AND PHILIP ENGLISH

The story of Mary and Philip English intersects with New York history only briefly during the infamous Salem Witch trials. Mary English née Hollingsworth was the daughter of William and Eleanor Hollingsworth, a wealthy family in the town of Salem. The Hollingsworth family arrived in Salem in 1635, when Mary's grandfather Richard was granted five hundred acres of land "where he can find it."[307] Richard Hollingsworth owned a shipyard on the south of Salem's Neck, where he became the first shipbuilder in the area. William inherited his father's large estate and respectability in the region. However, in 1674, the Hollingsworth family fell from grace and lost most of their fortune. Mary's mother, Eleanor, had to take over as manager of the family-owned Blue Anchor Tavern, which was located near the Hollingsworth shipyard. Eleanor was an unfavorable character, often flaunting family ties to the Crown and never leaving home without her personal servant.[308] One Blue Anchor Tavern customer complained that Eleanor was a "black-mouthed witch and a thief."[309] Mary was a talented weaver, as would be expected of her for the period, and a sampler of hers can still be viewed today at the Peabody Essex Museum, formerly Essex Institute.[310] In time, she would take over as proprietor of the Blue Anchor Tavern.[311] Mary's parents greatly desired her to marry into wealth, presumably to restore their family finances, and tried to set her up with suitable gentlemen that they approved of. While her father, William, was in Virginia for business sometime in 1674, he wrote home to his wife that he found a good husband for Mary. Eleanor replied that he shouldn't waste his time because she had already given Mary (twenty) to young Philip English (twenty-three). The two were officially married by 1675. Unfortunately, two years later, Mary's father was lost at sea and presumably died. Eleanor died in 1689, yet her reputation persisted and she was accused of witchcraft again two years after her death.

Samplers (*left*) made by Mary Hollingworth, married on July 1, 1676, to Philip English. *The New York Public Library Digital Collections.*

Philip English was born on July 30, 1651, on the island of Jersey located in the English Channel. His actual name was Philip L'Anglois, and he was the son of a wealthy merchant family with connections to the powerful De Carterets. His godfather was Sir Philip De Carteret, and it is presumed Philip English's mother was also a De Carteret.[312] These connections to the De Carteret family would prove financially fruitful on his arrival to America and the establishment of his trading company. Philip arrived in Salem likely in 1674 and bought property adjoining the Hollingsworth family. He made a fortune from shipping over families from Jersey to work as indentured servants in Salem; many of these families built homes on his property. After his marriage to Mary, they constructed an impressive house in 1683 called the "40 peaked house"—a flashy display of wealth with even the cellar having plastered walls.[313] The house has since been demolished but would have sat at the corner of Essex and English Streets in Salem. A year later, in 1684, Eleanor Hollingsworth gave Mary the Blue Anchor Tavern.[314] Philip's display of wealth stirred jealousy around Salem, and when combined with his litigious history, Mary's haughty demeanor and the disagreeable character of his late mother-in-law, this made the English family a prime target during the Salem Witch Trials. While Mary was described as having a sort-of superiority complex, Philip was described as sometimes impulsive and bad-tempered but generous and kind to the poor. In 1689, King William's War began creating a growing fear of the French in the colonies. Since Jersians hailed from French backgrounds, suspicion surrounded them. Many women in Salem who married Jersian men quickly found themselves accused of witchcraft.[315] Furthermore, Philip was an Anglican and made no effort to become Puritan, as was prevalent in the New England colonies.[316] As perhaps the wealthiest man in Salem, he aligned himself with the Porter family faction of Salem, a rival to the Putnam family, who controlled most of Salem. On March 8, 1692, Philip and several Porters were elected as town selectmen.[317] This too, made him and his wife targets for accusation.

In 1692, Mary was formally accused by Ann Putnam, Mercy Lewis and Mary Walcott, and on April 21 the town sheriff arrived at the English household with a warrant for Mary's arrest. Comically, the English family had retired for the night and—likely because of their wealth and social status— were able to postpone Mary's arrest until the next morning so that she could sleep, have breakfast and make arrangements for her children.[318] Mary was taken to prison and held for eight days, until Philip was also accused by Ann Putnam, Mercy Lewis, Mary Walcott, Abigail Williams and Susannah Sheldon. Philip had consistently visited Mary in prison to comfort her before his arrest. Susannah Sheldon stated that Philip English's specter, while she was in church, would step over the pew and pinch Susannah. Further, she stated that Philip was walking down the road with a "black man wearing a high crowned hat on his head" holding a book, and they wanted her to touch said book, claiming Philip referred to the man as her God.[319] The following day, this torment persisted to the point where Philip reportedly threatened to kill Susannah if she didn't sign the book.

Philip disappeared shortly before his arrest warrant was issued on May 2. However, Philip was unable to be located and a second warrant was issued in Boston on May 6 with the belief he may have fled there. His disappearance only made matters worse, and on May 12 more witchcraft complaints were filed against Mary. Shortly after, Susannah Sheldon further complained that the ghost of Joseph Rabson appeared to her for help, stating Philip English has drowned him to death while they were out at sea. At the same time, Philip's specter was threatening to cut her legs off if she were to listen to Joseph Rabson's ghost.[320] Philip's specter also threatened to kill ten folks in Boston if he were arrested. Philip emerged from hiding, was arrested and was sent back to Salem on May 30. On June 1, Mary English was one of several who accused Mary Warren (the oldest accuser of the Salem Witch Trial girls) of lying in court. The following day, the girls retaliated, with Susannah Sheldon taking the lead, by stating Bridget Bishop, Giles Corey and Mary English had visited her, and Bishop had implored her to sign her name in a book. Mary English's apparition, at this time, had a yellow bird in her bosom. When Susannah refused, they all took turns biting her. The next day, these apparitions tried again to get her to sign—this time Philip English was there as well—and she once again refused. That night, the apparitions tried again, this time Mary English proclaiming she had been a witch for twenty years.[321]

Philip and Mary knew things were not faring too well with their case. While imprisoned at Boston, their social class afforded them certain liberties that not every prisoner had access to. The couple were allowed to leave prison if they wanted, as long as they returned by the agreed time. During one particular day, they attended the services of Revered Joshua Moody, who was an outspoken critic of the witchcraft hysteria and sympathized with the English family.[322] Reverend Moody's sermon cryptically included the passage of Matthew 10:23, "When they persecute you in this city, flee ye into another" (King James Version), and so, that night, Moody helped secure safe passage for the English family into New York.[323] After their escape, Sheriff Corwin seized the English family estate for his own profit.[324]

Once in New York, Philip and Mary English were welcomed into the home of Governor Benjamin Fletcher, where they stayed until the witchcraft hysteria subsided.[325] It is said that Philip English, taking pity on those who could not escape Salem, sent a shipment of provisions to the town so that those whose farms and markets were affected could find sustenance.[326] Unfortunately, Mary English died shortly after returning to Salem, possibly from childbirth. Philip remarried but never could escape the gossip and rumors of the accusations against him. Philip continued to fight to retrieve his stolen assets from Sheriff Corwin. One legend, although myth, claims Philip English stole Corwin's corpse, which had been temporarily stored in the Corwin family cellar, placing a lien on the body if his family wanted it back. Regardless, Philip remarried and lived out the rest of his days in Salem. Interestingly, Philip and Mary English's granddaughter Susannah married into the Hawthorne family, ancestors of Nathaniel Hawthorne, whose family history inspired his famous novel *House of the Seven Gables* (1851).

ELIZABETH CARY

Elizabeth and Nathaniel Cary were a wealthy couple from Charleston, Massachusetts, who, having heard some unfamiliar individual named Elizabeth was a witch, decided to travel to Salem to personally investigate the accusation. Elizabeth was born sometime in 1650 to Captain Augustine and Hannah Walker and in 1674 married Nathaniel Cary, a shipmaster and shipbuilder from Lancashire, Massachusetts.[327] Fortunately, Nathaniel Cary's personal accounts of his family's ordeal still exist today. In 1693, Cotton Mather published *Wonders of the Invisible World: Being an Account of the Tryals of Several Witches, Lately Executed in New-England* to proudly promote his contribution to the Salem Witch Trials. After the Salem hysteria, which Cotton Mather perpetuated, fizzled out, Robert Calef published a collection of letters from the victims of the witchcraft hysteria in a book he cleverly named *More Wonders of the Invisible World* (1697). The following account is a letter from Nathaniel Cary, published in Calef's book:

I, having heard some days that my Wife was accused of Witchcraft, being much disturbed at it, by advice, we went to Salem-Village, to see if the afflicted did know her. We arrived there, May 24th, it happened to be a day appointed for examination. Accordingly, soon after our arrival, Mr. Hawthorn and Mr. Corwin, etc. went to the meetinghouse, which was the place appointed for that work. The Minister began with prayer, and having taken care to get a convenient place, I observed, that the afflicted were two Girls of about Ten Years old, and about two or three others, of about eighteen. One of the girls talked most and could discern more than the rest. The prisoners were called in one by one, and as they came in were cried out of, etc. The prisoner was placed about 7 or 8 feet from the justices, and the accusers between the justices and them. The prisoner was ordered to stand right before the Justices, with an officer appointed to hold each hand, lest they should afflict them, and the prisoners eyes must be constantly on the Justices; for if they looked on the afflicted, they would either fall into their fits, or cry out of being hurt by them. After examination of the prisoners, who it was afflicted these girls, etc., they were put upon saying the lord's prayer, as a [sign] of their guilt. After the afflicted seemed to be out of their fits, they would look steadfastly on some one person, and frequently not speak; and then the Justices said they were struck dumb, and after a little time would speak again; then the Justices said to the accusers, which of you will go and touch the prisoner at the bar? Then, the most courageous would adventure, but before they had made three steps would ordinarily fall down as in a fit. The Justices ordered that they should be taken up and carried to the prisoner, that she might touch them; and as soon as they were touched by the accused, the Justices would say, they are well, before I could discern any alteration; by which I observed that the Justices understood the manner of it. Thus far I was only as a spectator, my wife also was there part of the time, but no notice taken of her by the afflicted, except once or twice they came to her and asked her name.

But I having an opportunity to Discourse Mr. Hale (with whom I had formerly acquaintance) I took his advice, what I had best to do, and desired of him that I might have an opportunity to speak with her that accused my wife; which be promised should be. I, acquainting him, that I reposed my trust in him.

Accordingly, he came to me after the examination was over, and told me I had now an opportunity to speak with the said accuser, named Abigail Williams, a girl of 11 or 12 Years old, but that we could not be in private at Mr. Parris's House, as he had promised me. We went therefore into the Ale house, where an Indian man attended us, who it seems was one of the afflicted; to him we gave some cider, be shewed several scars that seemed as if they hadn't been there long, and shewed them as done by Witchcraft, and acquainted us that his wife, who also was a Slave, was imprisoned for witchcraft. And now instead of one accuser, they all came in, who began to tumble down like swine, and then three women were called in to attend them. We in the Room were all at a stand, to see who they would cry out of; but in a short time they cried out, Cary; and immediately after a warrant was sent from the Justices to bring my wife before them, who were sitting in a chamber nearby, waiting for this.

Being brought before the Justices, her chief accusers were two Girls; my wife declared to the Justices, that she never had any knowledge of them before that day; she was forced to stand with her Arms stretched out. I did request that I might hold one of her hands, but it was denied me; then she desired me to wipe the tears from her eyes, and the sweat from her face, which I did. Then she desired she might lean herself on me, saying, she should faint.

Justice Hawthorn replied, she had strength enough to torment those persons, and she should have strength enough to stand. I, speaking something against their cruel proceedings, they commanded me to be silent, or else I should be turned out of the room. The Indian before mentioned, was also brought in, to be one of her accusers: being come in, he now (when before the Justices) fell down and tumbled about like a hog but said nothing. The Justices asked the girls, who afflicted the Indian? they answered she (meaning my wife) and now lay upon him. The Justices ordered her to touch him, in order to his cure, but her head must be turned another way, lest instead of curing, she should make him worse, by her looking on him, her hand being guided to take hold of his. But the Indian took hold on her hand, and pulled her down on the floor, in a barbarous manner. Then his hand was taken off, and her hand put on his, and the cure was quickly wrought. I, being extremely troubled at their inhumane dealings, uttered a hasty speech [That God would take vengence on them and desired that God would deliver us out of the hands of unmerciful men.] *Then her mittimus was writ. I did with difficulty and charge obtain the liberty of a room, but no beds in it. If there had, could have taken but little rest. That night, she was committed to Boston Prison, but I obtained a*

Habeas Corpus to remove her to Cambridge Prison, which is in our County of Middlesex. Having been there one night, next morning the jailor put irons on her legs (having received such a command) the weight of them was about eight pounds. These irons and her other afflictions soon brought her into convulsive fits, so that I thought she would have died that night. I sent to intreat that the irons might be taken off, but all intreaties were in vain, if it would have saved her life, so that in this condition she must continue. The trials at Salem continuing on, I went thither, to see how things were there managed; and finding that the spectral evidence was there received, together with idle, if not malicious stories, against people's lives, I did easily perceive which way the rest would go. For the same evidence that served for one, would serve for all the rest. I acquainted her with her danger and that if she were carried to Salem to be tried, I feared she would never return. I did my utmost that she might have her trial in our own county, I with several others petitioning the Judge for it, and were put in hopes of it. But I soon saw so much, that I understood thereby it was not intended, which put me upon consulting the means of her escape. Which through the goodness of God was effected, and she got to Road-Island, but soon found herself not safe when there, by reason of the pursuit after her; from thence she went to New-York, along with some others that had escaped their cruel hands. Where we found his excellency Benjamin Fletcher Esq Governor, who was very courteous to us. After this, some of my goods were seized in a friend's hands, with whom I had left them, and myself imprisoned by the Sheriff, and kept in custody half a day, and then dismissed. But to speak of their usage of the prisoners, and their inhumanity shewn to them, at the time of their execution, no sober Christian could bear. They had also trials of cruel mockings, which is the more, considering what a people for religion, I mean the profession of it, we have been, Those that suffered being many of them church-members, and most of them unspotted in their conversation, till their adversary the devil took up this method for accusing them.

Per Nathaniel Cary

May 24ᵗʰ 1692[328]

After the Salem witch hysteria died down, Elizabeth and Nathaniel Cary ultimately returned to Charlestown, where they lived out the rest of their days. Nathaniel Cary's name often appears on lists of accused individuals during the Salem Witch Trials, but it's likely he was never named as a witch. However, it is certain he surely suffered alongside his wife the through the trials as well as what legacies or rumor surrounded the couple in the following years.

14

WINIFRED KING BENHAM
AND DAUGHTER

T he story of Winifred King Benham and her daughter Winifred Jr. begins in Wallingford, Connecticut, just before the turn of the eighteenth century. In fact, this was the last known recorded witch trial of the seventeenth century within this region. Winifred's mother, Mary, had been accused in Boston in 1656. This case is particularly unique, as it may have been the only instance in which three generations of the same family were brought to trial on witchcraft charges in three separate legal actions over the course of fifteen-plus years.[329]

Tracing Winifred Sr.'s lineage has proven a difficult task for many genealogists, but it is generally agreed on that she was born about 1639 in England and was the daughter of Mary King Hale (or Hayle) née Williams and her first husband (surname King), identity unknown. Discussion of Winifred's mother, Mary, is necessary in order to understand why and the extent to which this family was plagued by witchcraft gossip. Mary Williams King Hale was born sometime between 1606 and 1608, was married and widowed twice, and it is presumed that she had more than one child based on genealogical research.[330] In 1654, Mary appeared in Boston, and her brother Hugh Williams endorsed Mary to assure the courts of Boston that she would not become a charge of the town, indicating that she was likely widowed. In 1656, both Mary and her seventeen-year-old daughter Winifred King provided testimony in a property dispute involving Mary's brother. Winifred married Joseph a year later and relocated to Wallingford, Connecticut. Winifred's husband, Joseph, was one of Wallingford's earliest settlers, first arriving in Dorchester, Massachusetts, in 1630, marrying Winifred King from Boston in 1657, then creating a home together in Wallingford by 1670.[331] Joseph and Winifred's home was located somewhere south of Center Street, on the east side of Main Street.[332] By the 1680s, Mary Hale was a grandmother of Winifred's fourteen children and certainly kept busy with grandmotherly duties. For some time, Winifred's daughter and fourth-oldest child, Joanna Benham, had been staying at her grandmother Mary's house in Boston. At the time, a local mariner named Michael Smith was lodging at Mary's home and developed feelings for young Joanna. Mary did not approve of this relationship and quite possibly may have meddled and persuaded Joanna to refuse any advances from Smith. These details we may never truly know. However, Michael did give up his interest in Joanna and began courting a woman named Margaret Ellis instead. Michael told his new sweetheart that the reason his romance failed with Joanna was due to bewitchment at the hands of her grandmother Mary Hale. Michael claimed Mary bewitched him once while he was at the Isles of Shoals, another time while he was in Bilboa and at a separate occasion "transported" him to Dorchester in the company of an entire witch coven.[333] To further support these claims, Margaret conducted a traditional witchcraft divination experiment in which she collected Michael's urine in a bottle and observed Mary move about frantically when the bottle was capped, but when the cap was removed, she stopped moving. Unfortunately, Michael soon after died under mysterious circumstances and Margaret Ellis accused Mary of murder by witchcraft. Mary's trial occurred in 1680/81, and nineteen-year-old Joanna testified in support of her grandmother. Joanna stated, "Margaret Ellis told me that I and my grandmother Hale was the cause of his death and she hoped in the lord to see my grandmother Hale burned before she went out of the country and I would not be long first."[334] Margaret never got the satisfaction of watching Mary burn, as Mary disappeared from court records before the trial concluded and may have possibly fled to live with her daughter Winifred in Wallingford.

It is important to note that during this period, everyone in the community was obligated to self-regulate their neighborhoods to some degree and report slanderous or malicious activities to the authorities. This social obligation is a repeated theme in many of the witchcraft accusations throughout the seventeenth century. Back in Wallingford, in 1691, Winifred's husband, Joseph, had issues with the selectmen of Wallingford and spoke out, saying they were unfit for the job.[335] These public criticisms were promptly reported to local officials. Criticism of elected officials or offices of authority was politically and culturally unacceptable during this period.[336] Quickly, Joseph Benham was put on trial on June 15, 1691, at the county court in New Haven:

> *Joseph Benham of Wallingford presented for speaking words in Reproach against the townsmen (selectmen) of Wallingford vizt (namely) that they were no more fit for townsmen than dogs which was upon the last Tuesday in April and was now proved against him in court by 3 witnesses and the substance of the accusation confessed by himself for which he was fined to pay 5 *8 into the County treasury before the 1ˢᵗ of November, next for his so traducing and vilifying the said townsmen.*[337]

Joseph Benham appeared in court records again the next year, on July 25, 1692, at the New Haven County Court on behalf of a summons for a complaint against him.[338] A neighbor named Goodwife Hannah Parker had casually accused Winifred of witchcraft, presumably in association to her mother's own witchcraft suspicion and not fully realizing the severe implications of this accusation. Infuriated, Joseph threatened to load his gun with two bullets and shoot Goody Parker if she stepped foot in his house ever again. This rageful response was witnessed and reported by Sarah Howe Sr. and Abigaile Atwater, who attested to the event. The court then ordered Joseph "to be bound" (pay a sort of collateral) so that no harm would come to Goodwife Hannah Parker; her husband, Joseph Parker; and their family. The court then planned to meet next in November, when Joseph would be released of his collateral.[339] This accusation coincided with the witch hysteria in Salem, which gripped Massachusetts and surely dominated most conversations in New England and New York at the time. As gossip ruminated, Winifred Benham found herself at the center of suspicion for every little accident or mishap around the town. Several townsfolk, such as Hannah Parker, Deacon Hall and Anna Street, approached Reverend Samuel Street for guidance and, together, reported a formal complaint against Winifred Benham to the county court.[340] The county court advised the reverend and several complainants to consider the severity of their accusations and that the court would examine the matter closer at its next convening in November. This cautious approach to the multiple accusations was likely due to the ongoing Salem Witch Trials; the colonies were greatly reconsidering their position on witchcraft while witnessing the chaos happening not too far away.[341]

When the county court reconvened in New Haven on November 2, 1692, Winifred Benham was examined on suspicion of witchcraft. The

Samuel Street House. *Google Earth.*

court heard the testimonies of her neighbors as well as Winifred's rebuttal in which she denied any knowledge of the complaints or wrongdoing. The court decided that there were not sufficient grounds for conviction and moved to dismiss the case. However, the court advised Winifred to consider and reflect on the suspicions against her and that if further accusations were reported then she could expect to be brought to trial.[342] Winifred Sr. was checked for witches' marks/a witch's teat at her first trial in New Haven and possibly both requested and underwent the water test.[343] This verdict did not appease the townsfolk, and for the next five years, every little misfortune was blamed on Winifred. The townsfolk now expanded the controversy to include Winifred's thirteen-year-old daughter Winifred Jr., the youngest of Winifred Benham's fourteen children.[344] By then, Winifred Sr. was likely fifty-seven or fifty-eight years old.[345] These suspicions culminated on August 31, 1697, when the neighbors once again filed complaint against Winifred and her daughter.[346]

Winifred Benham Sr. was accused of witchcraft for a second time at the Superior Court in Hartford, Connecticut, in August 1697. The accusers represented at this trial were Ebenezer Clark, Joseph Royse and John Moss Jr., who testified that Sarah Clark (daughter of Ebenezer Clark), John Moss III (son of John Moss Jr.) and Elizabeth Lathrop were physically harmed by the apparitions and witchcraft of Winifred Benham Sr. and Winifred Benham Jr. or "by the Devil in their shapes" and demanded that the court examine the accused.[347] Unfortunately, the preponderance of evidence against the Benhams was too strong to ignore or dismiss, and the court ordered Joseph Benham to pay twenty-one pounds for their appearance and for them to be jailed until the next convening of the court in October. The courts also made note that a young child died with suspicious spots on the its body and that Benham also had spots on her body that vanished quickly.[348] On October 7, 1697, the Court of Assizes met in Hartford, and prosecutor Daniel Clark argued that Winifred Benham Sr. and Winifred Benham Jr. of Wallingford had made dealings with Satan and, through this relationship, had been causing mischief around the town of Wallingford, hurting numerous people and disturbing the peace. However, the jury was perplexed by the case and the politically charged atmosphere of witchcraft in the New England colonies and could not reasonably argue for the authenticity of the accusations.[349] Winifred Sr. was acquitted of the witchcraft charges due to only spectral evidence used against her in testimonies. Her daughter was also acquitted, and both fled to New York.[350] It is also presumed that, if she hadn't already passed away, Winifred's mother, Mary Hale, may have accompanied her daughter and granddaughter to New York.[351] Whether Winifred Sr./ and/or her mother, Mary, lived out their days on Staten Island is unknown.

Elizabeth Alice Austen House, 2 Hyland Boulevard, Rosebank, Richmond County, New York. *National Park Service.*

However, it is likely Winifred and her husband, Joseph, remained on Staten Island, with Joseph passing away in 1703.[352] Also, several Benham daughters married men from Staten Island, which gives some insight into Winifred's life on Staten Island. In 1696, Winifred's daughter Anna Benham and Anna's husband, Lambert Johnson, had a daughter (named Winifred) baptized at the Dutch Church of Staten Island.[353] It was likely this daughter to whom Winifred Sr. fled with her younger children,[354] though Winifred Sr. may possibly have lived with her other daughter Sara and Sara's husband, Jacob Johnson. This house is still extant and known locally as the Alice Austen House, receiving its moniker from later resident Elizabeth Alice Austen, the well-known Staten Island photographer. Winifred Jr. also remained on Staten Island, marrying local Evert Van Namen.[355] Attesting to the character and legacy of Winifred King Benham, we can assume that she may have had a rough relationship with Wallingford neighbors, but as for her family, we know that she had an astounding fourteen children with Joseph, whatever that may say of their marriage, and two of the Benham children named a child after their mother, indicating that they were likely fond of her.[356]

15

THE SEVENTEENTH CENTURY REVISITED

In this section, we have reviewed the lives of twenty-one individuals accused or suspected of witchcraft, either within the boundaries of present-day New York or in an adjacent colony, escaping to New York as a refugee from the law. What we realize from these individual accounts is that New York, for the most part, did in fact have an extensive history of witchcraft, although overshadowed by the relatively massive scale of accusations in New England at the time. Further, we find that the sentiments of colonial New York authorities, regarding the crime of witchcraft, were much more relaxed than the Puritan magistrates of New England, having released all those who had been accused, while finding creative ways to still please the frightened and aggravated townsfolk who would be accusers.

We find that the common narrative of witch accusations as a result of a Puritan belief system may not neatly fit the mold of history as we are often led to believe. Let us review the aforementioned cases. The earliest instance of witchcraft recorded by Europeans was the case of Isaac Jogues, Réne Goupil and John de Lalande, all three religious missionaries attempting to colonize and religiously convert Native American communities. The kinetic and often hostile relationship between Europeans and Native Americans, the strange behavior of the visiting European missionaries and the unintentional spread of disease from missionaries to Native American communities provided enough justification to convince these communities that evil was among them and that they needed to take action. This ultimately resulted in the three missionaries getting their skulls cleaved with an axe, the common remedy for a problematic witch/murderer in Native American communities of the time.

Soon we have the coastal Algonquian sachems attempting to pull the puppet strings of colonial magistrates, seizing all opportunities to dominate enemy tribes. Uncas, sachem of the Mohegan, reported to the Connecticut Colony magistrates that Sachem Poggatacut was employing witchcraft with murderous intent, and soon after Sachem Wyandanch, or at least an agent of Wyandanch, was also accused. Although these events took place under the aegis of the Puritan colonial government, we see here no legal action being taken by the Puritans. Meanwhile, the Lenape people of Staten Island became convinced that Cornelis Melyn had sold them defective weapons, was trying to poison them and was likely a sorcerer supported by the European Staten Island settlers. Cornelis, although an unsavory character himself, was forced to flee with his family to the Connecticut Colony. Afterward, we met Elizabeth Garlick, whose case was excused, with her life and freedom to return to normalcy in her hometown. Her neighbors were warned not to cause her further trouble. Mary Wright Andrews, was accused only of Quakerism and not of witchcraft at all, although accused centuries after her passing by an overzealous historian. Judith Varleth Bayard found refuge in New York, through help from powerful family friends, from Connecticut Colony accusations with Goodwife Ayres following behind. The Hall family, although residing in an English settlement, stood trial in the Dutch-dominated courts in the last days of the Dutch New Netherland colony. Their punishment also resolved relatively undramatically, with the Halls being excised from their village and forced to relocate to a different area within the colony, more so to appease their neighbors than to actually punish the Halls. Katherine Harrison was accused in the Connecticut Colony and after her banishment was accused once more in Westchester (town), an English settlement nestled in Dutch New York, based solely on the gossip that preceded her. Maes Cornelis's case was squashed early and didn't progress past slander—accusing him of turning to the devil. Hannah Travally's accusation also occurred in an English settlement dominated by a mostly Dutch-influenced court and resulted with the punishment of her accuser, paying no credibility to any relationship between her and the supernatural. For Goody Miller, the English family, the Cary family and the Benham family, these folks were refugees who found temporary and/or permanent shelter within New York's borders during the Salem Witch Trial period. While only the English and Cary families were accused by Salem Village accusers, Goody Miller and the Benhams' accusers were certainly influenced by the witchcraft hysteria radiating through the New England colonies at this time (1692–93).

There are many commonalities with these seventeenth-century accounts. Primarily, each instance of witchcraft accusation takes place during a time of community stress. During this century, Native American accusers and/ or accused, were only males, while Europeans accused of witchcraft were predominantly woman. In the few cases where men were accused, it was always because of their relationship with an accused woman—their wives— although Maes Cornelis is an exception, if he could even qualify as a witchcraft suspect at all is debatable. Nevertheless, witchcraft as a punishable crime under Euro-American law had seen its height in the northeastern colonies, and skepticism by legal authorities had begun to take root. As we move into the eighteenth century, we will see less legal prosecution and more suspicion and folklore than this present chapter in history.

II

EIGHTEENTH CENTURY

I have gone out, a possessed witch,
haunting the black air, braver at night;
dreaming evil, I have done my hitch
over the plain houses, light by light:
lonely thing, twelve-fingered, out of mind.
A woman like that is not a woman, quite.
I have been her kind.

—*"Her Kind" by Anne Sexton (*To Bedlam and Part Way Back, *1960)*

16

INTRODUCTION TO
THE EIGHTEENTH CENTURY

The Scientific Revolution transformed into the Age of Enlightenment in the eighteenth century and so some thought the Western world cured of its witchcraft beliefs, at least in the learned community of ivory tower intellectuals and judiciary magistrates. New York was still under the legal authority of the British Empire for the greater part of the eighteenth century and still subject to British laws and opinion. In 1735, the British Empire passed the Witchcraft Act, which shifted the crime of witchcraft from a supernatural threat against British citizens to a threat against the new enlightened status of British society.[357] *Claiming* witchcraft was now the crime, more so than being the presumed cause of a horrible event. Witchcraft was now incorporated into the realm of superstition, and those who claimed to practice witchcraft or be affected by it were seen as charlatans and subject to penalty. The eighteenth century saw superstition approached with scientific intrigue and each supernatural phenomenon questioned. However, just because the law had changed, as well as the philosophies of educated elite, doesn't mean communities tossed away these deeply rooted beliefs and anxieties. The fear of witchcraft still persisted among many different New York communities, and both suspicion and accusation continued, whether the accusers could take some legal action against the suspected person or not. Witchcraft historians often find that jurisdiction was not the only cause of witchcraft accusations. In fact, times of societal stress often foster community anxieties and mistrust and have been theorized as contributing factors to witchcraft accusations.

The political and social environment of the eighteenth century included many types of social stress on the people living within New York. Cultural and political landscapes were rapidly changing from the onslaught of the French and Indian War engagements, Christian proselytizing pushing against the revitalization of Haudenosaunee traditions and the American Revolutionary War. Political borders and boundaries were changing, waves of European immigrants were arriving to the Americas and community identities were being negotiated and molded into the forms we are familiar with and operate within today. Nevertheless, people persisted in accusing and suspecting each other of witchcraft, though not at the height we observed in the seventeenth century. To the Euro-American colonists, America was still the frontier and with it persisted the fear of the unknown.

17

UNNAMED WOMAN NO. 1

Alleged Bewitcher of Aquendero's Son

This first witchcraft accusation in the eighteenth century shares similarities with the first instance of witchcraft accusations in the previous century (See the Jesuit Sorcerers chapter). Both instances involved the Mohawk Nation, connections to the Jesuits and the spread of disease and occurred during a time of political uncertainty. In this case, an Indigenous woman from Canada associated with the French Jesuits arrived in the Onondaga Nation, and after some unspecified time of suspicion and rumor, she was executed by a Mohawk man for the crime of witchcraft.

This transcribed text is from the Earl of Bellomont in correspondence to the "Lords of Trade and Plantations" and gives a brief account of the events that transpired:

[To the Lords of Trade and Plantations,]

Aquendero, the chief Sachem of the Onondaga Nation, who was prolocutor for all the Five Nations as the Conference I had two years ago at Albany, has been forced to fly from thence, and come and live on Coll. Schuyler's land near Albany. Aquendero's son is poisoned, and languishes, and there is a sore broke out on one of his sides, out of which there comes handfuls of hair, so that they reckon he has been bewitched, as well as poisoned. I met with an old story from the gentlemen of Albany, which I think worth relating. Decannissore, one of the Sachems of the Onondagas, married one of the Praying Indians in Canada (by praying Indians is meant such are

instructed by the Jesuits). This woman was taught to poison as well as to pray. The Jesuits had furnished her with so subtle a poison and taught her a Legerdemain in using it, so that whoever she had a mind to poison, she would drink to them a cup of water, and let drop the poison from under her nail (which are always very long, for the Indians never pare them) into the cup. This woman was so true a disciple to the Jesuits, that she has poisoned a multitude of our Five Nations that were best affected to us. She lately coming from Canada in company of some of our Indians, who went to visit their relations in that country who have taken sides with the French; and, there being among others a Protestant Mohawk (a proper goodly young man), him this woman poisoned so that he died two days journey short of Albany, and the Magistrates of that town sent for his body and gave it a Christian burial. The woman comes to Albany, where some of the Mohawks happened to be, and among them a young man nearly related to the man that had been poisoned, who spying the woman, cries out with great horror, that there was that beastly woman that had poisoned so many of their friends, and it was not fit she should live any longer in this world to do more mischief; and so made up to her with a club beat out her brains.
[Earl of Bellomont, 1700][358]

During this period of history, the French were persistent in their desire for Haudenosaunee land, and violence became common between the French and the Mohawk starting in 1609. Tensions ultimately ended after 154 years, when the Mohawk drove out the French from Haudenosaunee territory in 1763.[359] The Haudenosaunee people were suspicious of French-aligned visitors to their communities during this period, and the unnamed woman's association with an Onondaga sachem would have surely raised eyebrows and inspired gossip. The preceding text from the Earl of Bellomont is the only extant record of this account, and not much is known about life of this accused woman. However, there are some clues to figuring out more details to her story. As the Earl of Bellomont writes, the Haudenosaunee people in the New York region would often travel across the Canadian border to visit family. This unnamed woman traveled back with a party returning from Canada and married an Onondaga sachem named Decannissore. Her connection to the French Jesuits of Canada may have already made Onondaga neighbors suspicious of her arrival, and surely, she would have been seen as an outsider. If we presume that the French Jesuits traveling through Mohawk villages in the seventeenth century spread diseases to the unsuspecting Native Americans, then perhaps this is what we are also observing in this event at the turn of the century. This unnamed woman may have made her neighbors uneasy, considering that the Mohawks had a history with Jesuit-connected "sorcery."

Two particularities stand out when reading about Aquendero's son's symptoms. One, the description of a sore on his body filled with "handfuls of hair" could allude to puss-filled sores commonly caused from the smallpox virus. Further, the other symptoms of "poisoning" may describe smallpox symptoms of fever, chills and vomiting associated with the virus. This would be concurrent with the ongoing and persistent smallpox epidemics through the seventeenth and eighteenth centuries. Attributing sickness to microscopic pathogens was unknown and ascribing this misfortune as bewitchment was easier to accept and seemingly easier to resolve. Kill the witch; end the suffering. Once more, in this account, we see hints to some relationship between European herbalism/Western medicines and the accused. The accused woman is rumored to have learned how to poison from the Jesuits and employed the tactics and will of her nefarious European masters. While this book primarily consults an imperfect historical record, it's possible that this accused woman was an asymptomatic carrier of smallpox and had spread the disease in a like manner of the Jesuits. If this is the case, it may explain the symptoms of Aquendero's son and the reason for this woman's prosecution and murder.

18

UNNAMED WOMAN NO. 2 (1710–1720)

Within the pages of a Staten Island history is a brief reference to a woman accused of witchcraft in the early eighteenth century.[360] This woman is not named, and all we know is the punishment she received. In the neighborhood of Hollins Hook lived an older woman who was believed to be in league with Satan, causing mischief in her community.[361] Her neighbors would hang horseshoes over their doors, as they were believed to ward away the malevolent apparitions of witches intending to do harm.

This unfortunate woman was an early victim of the community's newly constructed whipping post, erected in 1710. This whipping post was located "on the elevation between Saint Andrews church and the roadway leading up the steep side of Richmond Hill on or near the spot where the public school building now stands."[362] The existence and use of this whipping post persisted until about 1824, after which its history is obscured.[363]

Example of a whipping post. *Wikimedia Commons / Public domain.*

19

AUNTY GREENLEAF

The Aunty Greenleaf (1727)[364] account is one story found only in New York folklore. It was first recorded in 1979 and had been repeated/altered through the ages.[365] The story of Aunty Greenleaf is set in Brookhaven, New York, at an unspecified time in the superstitious past. Legend says that Aunty Greenleaf was an old witch who lived by herself outside the village. She had a profound knowledge of herbal remedies, which she sold to the townsfolk. This arcane knowledge resulted in a local suspicion of her potential malevolent intentions. One prominent member of the community had seen her in a dream and the next morning found their daughter to be sick with a fever and thereby blamed Greenleaf for the cause.[366] Another time, a farmer argued with Greenleaf, and shortly after his hogs died off one by one. Once again, Aunty Greenleaf was the alleged cause.[367]

These suspicions culminated during a series of strange sightings of an all-white deer within the forest. These bizarre deer sightings coincided with a string of unexplained livestock deaths and reports of butter that would not churn. Freaky occurrences prompted the local townsfolk to gather into a hunting party, track down and shoot this white deer and end the torment experienced throughout the town of Brookhaven. The townsfolk succeeded in locating the notorious white deer, but the creature quickly fled after the initial shots had been fired, leaving the hunters to speculate the creature was impervious to bullets. A determined farmer melted his family silver and cast silver bullets to terminate this cursed deer. The hunting party reconvened and this time was successful in the hunt, hitting the white deer—although

A witch holding a plant in one hand and a fan in the other (with symbols on her clothing). Woodcut, circa 1700–20. *Wellcome Collection.*

it did not fall dead but instead used its remaining energy to escape from the eyes of its enemies. While tracking the injured white deer, the hunters were distracted by wails of pain coming from Aunty Greenleaf's cabin. They entered and found her to be in immense pain in bed and called for the

A white deer. Photograph by Bert de Tilly. *Wikimedia Commons.*

doctor to arrive and help. The town doctor examined her and found silver bullets lodged in her spine, indicating Greenleaf was likely the white deer they had shot. Aunty Greenleaf expired shortly afterward, and the white deer was never seen in Brookhaven again.

This legend bears striking similarities to several others[368] from the region. For example, there is a Native American witchcraft legend concerning a cattle herder and a local begrudged woman with elements similar to the Aunty Greenleaf story. The cattle farmer noticed his herd was being disturbed throughout the night and were exhausted during the day. He stayed awake at night to investigate and found a goose had been disturbing the herd night after night. He loaded his gun and fired on the goose with no success and repeated this hunt for several nights. He finally obtained a silver bullet and clipped the goose in one of its wings. The next morning, he awoke to the news that a woman he had a grudge against had a terrible arm injury and soon realized she was a witch.[369] In the Aunty Greenleaf story, the creature is a white deer, another spiritual animal in Native American legend.[370] Another similar story comes from Bridgehampton, New York, a coastal village on the southern fork of Long Island. In this story, an unnamed farm was presumably cursed so that every harvest of hay was soaked by rain before entering the barn. The workmen, being superstitious, prepared a gun with silver bullets in the event a malevolent creature (likely a witch's familiar) would appear. When they began to start the day's work, a black cat appeared in the field. One of the men grabbed a gun and just barely clipped the cat with a bullet; it limped away. For the first time, the hay harvest entered the barn dry. For the following few days after the shooting, a local elderly woman, often suspected of being a witch, was not seen. When she finally returned to the public eye, the old woman appeared to be injured and walking with a cane, which seemingly validated those villagers who suspected her of being responsible for the cursed farm.[371] In many of these stories, the malevolent animal changes, but a defining marker is the use of a silver bullet or silver button[372] loaded into a musket to kill or injure the therianthropic witch.

Once more in a Seneca story do we follow similar events.

Witches could and did assume animal shapes.

On the Buffalo Reservation a man saw a "witch-woman" coming, with fire streaming from her mouth. Crossing a creek and obtaining his gun the man returned and saw a dog at no great distance resting its forefeet upon a log, and it had fire streaming from its mouth and nostrils.

The man fired at it and saw it fall, but as it was very dark, he dared not go near it; but on the following morning he went to the spot and saw where it had fallen, by the marks of blood from its wound. Tracking it by this means he followed its path until it had reached a bridge, where the woman's tracks took the place of the dog's tracks in the path. He followed the bloody trail to the Tonawanda Reservation, where he found the woman. She had died from the effect of the shot.[373]

Furthermore, like all great camp stories, this Aunty Greenleaf version contains kernels of truth and is worth examining for the study of witchcraft accusations in this region. First, the setting of this story is of particular interest to witchcraft history, as the early settlement of Brookhaven was located in present-day Setauket. Setauket should sound familiar, as it was the home of accused witches Mary and Ralph Hall in 1665, who likely inspired this myth. It is also likely that the events of Goody Garlick's case in East Hampton influenced some elements of the story and name of the antagonist, Aunty Greenleaf (the two-syllable title "Aunty" being similar to "Goody"). The original legend states that a "prominent citizen" dreamed of Greenleaf, and that after having this dream, their daughter had nearly died of a fever. This event bears striking similarities to the case of Goody Garlick, who was accused of bewitching and ultimately killing Lion Gardiner's daughter in East Hampton. Lastly, it should be noted that an actual woman named Elizabeth Gooking Greenleaf did in fact exist in New England between 1681 and 1762 and was certainly interested in herbal healing, as she is considered the first female pharmacist in the United States. However, Elizabeth Gooking Greenleaf resided in Cambridge, Massachusetts, not Brookhaven, New York, though news of her notoriety would surely have spread to New York during this period, as it challenged the patriarchal society of eighteenth-century New England. What's also important to note is that Elizabeth Greenleaf's legacy is obscured by a largely ignored field of research, and little has been written about her life as America's first female pharmacy owner. Whatever amalgamation of regional myths, parables and historical events created the Aunty Greenleaf story may never be known for certain but certainly lives on as a recognizable and influential element of witchcraft folklore here in New York.

20

BUCKINJEHILLISH

ll we know about Buckinjehillish (1730) comes from a short paragraph in the 1826 *A Narrative of the Life of Mrs. Mary Jemison* by James E. Seaver. Seaver transcribed his interviews with Mary Jemison (who we will discuss later), where Mrs. Jemison tells the story of several Indigenous people accused/suspected of witchcraft, including herself. Buckinjehillish's brief description is as follows:

> *The delectable story is told of Buckinjehillish, a very old Indian warrior, who angered the Council by saying that only the ignorant made war, but the wise men and the warriors did the fighting. He was accused of witchcraft for living so long, and because he could not show some reason why he had not died before, he was sentenced to be tomahawked by a boy on the spot—which was accordingly done.*[374]

This brief account is merely a transcription from oral history, and we may never know the details of Buckinjehillish's life or if further reasoning was provided to justify his execution. This account derives from a time when witch accusations were all too ubiquitous among the Iroquois and during a period of Western historiography when Native Americans were particular invisible to Euro-American authors. The interest of Mary Jemison, a white woman raised by Native Americans, offers historical clues, by association, to the extent of witchcraft beliefs among Iroquois communities during this particular period.

21

MARY NEWTON

There is not much known about Mary Newton's life, save for a brief passage hidden on the last page of the Islip town council minutes record book of the eighteenth century. The report states that an individual named Clemson Morris filed a "scandalous" report against Mary Newton, to which Mary was ordered to have her body inspected for any unusual marks. Clemson later recanted his accusation and apologized for the false report:

Scandalous Report
August ye 2 Anno Dom 1737
Whereas there has been a Scandalous Report Raised by Clement Morrise Junior against Mary Newton Daughter of John Newton: and to End all Controversy ye said Mary Newton has been Searched by Elizabeth Phillips and She has Declared before us that the said Mary Newton is in her Proper Shape & nothing Deferent from other Women upon any account but what is usual and ye said Clement Morrise has Acknowledge that He Raised a false Report against her ye said Mary Newton and is very sorry for it.
Witness by us
George Phillips
William Green
Elizabeth Phillips
Enter September ye 24 1737
by me George Phillips, Clark (clerk.)[375]

Above: Town of Islip First Minute Book, town records of the eighteenth century. *Photograph by author.*

Opposite: *Examination of a Witch* by Tompkins Harrison Matteson (1853). *Wikimedia Commons / Public domain.*

The report that Mary's body was inspected for an unusual marking is what made this entry suspicious at first glance. There is no explicit mention of witchcraft, or any crime as a matter of fact, but the context clues have provided insight for historians. The entry itself seemed to have been intentionally buried in the record book after several blank pages, implying that the author of this entry did not intend for any casual review of the town records to immediately show that entry. The title of the entry as a "Scandalous Report" and the fact it was recorded at all indicate that it was a serious matter at the time, regardless of the event's details. The scandalous nature of the event is presumed to be witchcraft, considering the political atmosphere involving occult crime nearly thirty years after the Salem Witch Trials; officials would have been cautious to pursue a case of this nature.[376]

Mary's body was inspected and found to be in "proper shape and nothing different from other women upon any account than what is usual." Islip Town historian George Muckenbeck has linked this remark to the traditional belief of the witch's teat, which, as explained in previous sections, references a third nipple on a witch's body from which a familiar drinks blood from to receive energy and wreak havoc on the community.[377] Mary was excused from any suspicion, as a witch's teat was not identified on her body. What's more conclusive is that the accuser Clemson Morris

Newton Family Cemetery. *Photograph by author.*

never appears in the town records again after that entry, suggesting that he was exiled from the town.[378] This presumption makes the most sense, since Clemson's involvement in such an event and his admission of filing a false report would have certainly been reprimanded by local authorities. Unfortunately, there are no other known extant records of this event, and we may never know what fully transpired for Mary Newton in 1737. Further, Mary herself seems a bit elusive to the pages of history. The Newton family was extensive in the town of Islip, and the name Mary was widely used in the Newton family. The Newton Family Cemetery may be this particular Mary's resting place and is located at the corner of St. James Road and Ebzu Court in Lake Grove, New York.

22

MARY JEMISON

In 1758, twelve-year-old Mary Jemison was captured by French and Native American raiders in Pennsylvania. Her adoption into the Seneca tribe and subsequent life as a Seneca woman in New York would come to see her accused of witchcraft by her Indigenous neighbors. Many Seneca people were accused of and executed for witchcraft during her lifetime. Mary's story occurs during many historical events of particular importance, such as the French and Indian War and the American Revolution, which contribute the stressors and anxieties preceding witchcraft accusations in American history.[379]

Mary Jemison's parents were Thomas and Jane Jemison of Scots-Irish origin, who sailed on the *William and Mary* out of Ireland in 1742–43. They immigrated for better prospects in America, leaving behind their ancestral homes in Europe. Mary was born during this cross-Atlantic journey. The ship arrived in Philadelphia, and the Jemison family set out to build their homestead in Marsh Creek, Pennsylvania, and begin their life in the New World. According to Mary, life was considerably quiet, simple and happy during her youth. Her mother would go on to have three more children—Matthew, Robert and Betsey—while enjoying life on the frontier. It wasn't until 1752 that the proverbial storm clouds began to roll over the Jemison family with traveling warnings of French and Native attacks on British American settlements. The French and Indian War was beginning, and the Jemisons' home was unfortunately in the path of conflict.

For nearly a century, French and allied Native American tribes had engaged British (and Dutch) forces allied with other Native American tribes for the conquest of land, natural resources that could help fuel European markets and dominant political power in America. In 1754, Native and British forces (including twenty-one-year-old Major George Washington) clashed against French and Native foes, leaving smoke and dead bodies in their wake, including Mary's uncle, who served in Washington's unit. The Jemison family relied completely on the protection provided by British forces and the hopes that these soldiers were close by if something were to happen. A system of forts was constructed in Pennsylvania to aid settlers during enemy raids, but these forts proved to be largely ineffective. The challenging terrain, dense forests and great distances between forts made it difficult for settlers to reach safety, especially considering how quick, and without warning, enemy ambushes were.[380]

Four years of anxiety passed until one precarious morning when a French/Native squad consisting of six Shawnee and four Frenchmen attacked the Jemison home, sacked what valuables they could find (mostly food) and captured the family. They marched the Jemisons off to be traded. One night along their journey, while the captives were eating, Mary's mother realized the unlikeliness of their survival and what awfulness was to follow. In her recollection, Mary states:

> As soon as I had finished my supper, an Indian took off my shoes and stockings and put a pair of moccasins on my feet, which my mother observed; and believing that they would spare my life, even if they should destroy the other captives, addressed me as near as I can remember in the following words:—"My dear little Mary, I fear that the time has arrived when we must be parted forever. Your life, my child, I think will be spared; but we shall probably be tomahawked here in this lonesome place by the Indians. O! how can I part with you my darling? What will become of my sweet little Mary? Oh! how can I think of your being continued in captivity without a hope of your being rescued? O that death had snatched you from my embraces in your infancy; the pain of parting then would have been pleasing to what it now is; and I should have seen the end of your troubles!—Alas, my dear! my heart bleeds at the thoughts of what awaits you; but, if you leave us, remember my child your own name, and the name of your father and mother. Be careful and not forget your English tongue. If you shall have an opportunity to get away from the Indians, don't try to escape; for if you do, they will find and destroy you. Don't forget, my little daughter, the prayers that I have learned you—say

Indians Attacking a Jamestown Home. Illustration from History of the Pilgrims and Puritans, Their Ancestry and Descendants; basis of Americanization *(1922) by Joseph Dillaway Sawyer.*

them often; be a good child, and God will bless you. May God bless you my child and make you comfortable and happy."[381]

Jane Jemison was right, as Mary and another little boy who had been captured from another family were led off away from the group. The next day, the captors rejoined, this time without Mary's parents and siblings. They were surely killed, and Mary's suspicions were soon confirmed when they reached their next camp site. One Native man built a big fire and took out a collection of bloody human scalps from his bag to stretch out on hoops and dry near the fire for preservation. Mary, recalling her trauma from twelve years old, said:

Having put the scalps, yet wet and bloody, upon the hoops, and stretched them to their full extent, they held them to the fire till they were partly dried and then with their knives commenced scraping off the flesh; and in that way they continued to work, alternately drying and scraping them, till they were dry and clean. That being done they combed the hair in the neatest manner, and then painted it and the edges of the scalps yet on the hoops, red. Those scalps I knew at the time must have been taken from our family

by the color of the hair. My mother's hair was red; and I could easily
distinguish my father's and the children's from each other. That sight was
most appalling; yet, I was obliged to endure it without complaining.

Mary and the boy were marched farther north until finally arriving at Fort Pitt, where they were traded to other Native American families. Mary was traded to a Seneca family and was raised as their own. From then on, she was given the name De-ge-wa-nus, meaning "pretty girl" or "pleasant good thing." It was as a Seneca woman that she lived the rest of her life.

Native American tribes at this place and time feared the threat of witches living among them. Jemison claims that Native American "witches" were executed by the Seneca nearly every year since she had been taken and adopted into the tribe (circa 1758). Her firsthand account underscores the fact that the ubiquity of American witchcraft accounts has been largely ignored when they don't center European victims. If we are to trust the words of Mary Jemison, or the biographer who transcribed her story in 1823, James Seaver, then the number of accused witches in New York State is presumably much greater than the accounts listed within this book.[382]

Mary married a Seneca man named Sheninjee, and together they lived peaceably and had a son named Thomas. As the seasons passed, Mary's adoptive family gradually made the move from their village south of present-day Pittsburgh, Pennsylvania, to a larger Seneca village along the Genesee River in New York near the city of Geneseo in Livingston County. The village was called Genishau, and soon Mary was convinced by her Seneca brothers to come live there with her husband and son. Sheninjee died of sickness before he could make it to Genishau to join his family. The years passed, and Mary married another man named Hiokatoo and had four daughters and two more sons. Through the years she had experienced many hardships imposed on the Seneca people both externally and internally. War, disease and famine troubled her and her community, and the fear of witchcraft permeated Seneca culture. Mary's own son John used the accusation of witchcraft to kill his older half brother Thomas, for which this murder was deemed justified in the eyes of the Seneca elders. Mary herself was accused but through one reason or another was spared. In Mary's own words, she summarized her struggles and legacies during her life:

It was believed for a long time, by some of our people, that I was a great
witch, but they were unable to prove my guilt, and consequently I escaped the
certain doom of those who are convicted of that crime which, by the Indians,

is considered as heinous as murder. Some of my children had light brown hair, and tolerable fair skin, which used to make some say that I stole them; yet as I was ever conscious of my own constancy, I never thought that anyone really believed that I was guilty of adultery. I have been the mother of eight children; three of whom are now living, and I have at this time thirty-nine grandchildren, and fourteen great-grandchildren, all living in the neighborhood of Genesee River, and at Buffalo. I live in my own house, and on my own land, with my youngest daughter, Polly, who is married to George Chongo, and has three children. My daughter Nancy, who is married to Billy Green, lived about 80 rods south of my house, and has seven children. My other daughter Betsey is married to John Green, has seven children, and resides 80

Illustration of Mary Jemison, by Harriet S. Caswell (1892). *Wikimedia Commons / Public domain.*

rods north of my house. Thus, situated in the midst of my children, I expect I shall soon leave the world, and make room for the rising generation. I feel the weight of years with which I am loaded and am sensible of my daily failure in seeing, hearing, and strength; but my only anxiety is for my family. If my family will live happily, and I can be exempted from trouble while I have to stay, I feel as though I could lay down in peace a life that has been checked in almost every hour, with troubles of a deeper dye, than are commonly experienced by mortals.[383]

Mary Jemison passed away in 1833, but her legacy of strength lives on, not only through her descendants but also through several statues and monuments dedicated to her in both New York and Pennsylvania. Her grave and a statue are in the Seneca Council Grounds, located near Letchworth State Park along the Genesee River, 6484 Park Road, Genesee Falls, NY 14427. The Livingston County Historical Society in Geneseo still has on display a woven basket made by Mary Jemison herself. There is another marker near her family's original homestead in Pennsylvania, located at 987–1173 Church Road, Orrtanna, PA 17353.

23

MARGARET TELFORD

T he place name Salem has become synonymous with American witchcraft, so it is therefore a particular curiosity that Salem, Massachusetts, was not the only Salem town in America to have a witch history. In fact, the village of Salem, New York, had its own witch trial in 1777, nearly eighty-five years after the notorious witch trials that we all learn about today. The name Salem derives from biblical Middle East origins and generally translates to mean "peace" (Hebrew *shalom*, Arabic *salaam*), not unlike Jerusalem, which means "city of peace." However, during the witch trial of Salem, New York, the towns original name wasn't exactly agreed on. Some settlers named it New Perth, while others preferred White Creek. It wasn't until 1786 (nine years after this particular witch trial) that the townsfolk agreed to name their town Salem. The woman accused of witchcraft in this account was named Margaret Telford,[384] and to properly understand her story, we must first discuss the history of Salem, New York.

The story of Salem starts in Scotland with Reverend Thomas Clark, a Presbyterian minister, a medical doctor and, for a period of time, a soldier. Reverend Clark served a large part of his career as a missionary in Ballybay, Northern Ireland, where he captivated the ears of an estimated 200 people with his sermons. After a series of unfortunate events, such as imprisonment for refusing to swear an oath that his religion prevented him from doing and losing his wife and son, he petitioned the presbytery to travel to America, which was granted to him. He left from Newry, Ireland, on May 10, 1764, and arrived in New York on July 28, 1764, on a vessel named *John* with a congregation of 300 settlers.[385] However, some controversy and disagreement split up the party, and only 140 went with Reverend Clark, while the other 160 traveled south to South Carolina. Reverend Clark's journey took him and 140 settlers up the Hudson River to the town of Stillwater, just north of Albany.

In 1765, Clark obtained twenty-five thousand acres of land, where Salem, New York, sits today, to establish a town, and he divided the land into 308 lots, a forest for public use and 3 lots set apart for the preacher and a schoolmaster.[386] These early settlers, temporarily stationed in Stillwater, worked together to construct their new village in Salem and, in doing so, also began to construct their town and community's identity.[387] Seven years after the town was constructed, Margaret and George Telford arrived in Salem. Latecomers as they were, they were entering a community that was already forged with the literal construction of the village's foundation as a settler community. The Telfords may have been initially perceived as outsiders who didn't endure the shared experience of cross-Atlantic travel as a community of religious pioneers, nor did they face the struggles of planning and building a town on the open frontier. Nevertheless, the Telfords were here in Salem and ready to settle down and live their lives. It is likely that an agent of Clark's presbytery recruited the Telfords back in Scotland, where they had been residing. Margaret was born in Scotland in 1725, while her husband, George Telford, was born in 1728, also in Scotland. In May 1772, they left Castletown, Roxburgh, Scotland, with five children, and tragically their infant son died along the journey. In August of that same year, they arrived in Salem. Upon their arrival, they initially sought shelter in an empty house near Fitch's Point before building their own house near East Greenwich.[388]

Historian John R. Henderson, a descendant of Margaret and a published authority on the Telford family history, provides two examples of George's strict adherence to the Sabbath. In one account, late one Saturday, George dropped off grain to the local miller to be ground. The next day, while George and his family were attending church service, the miller recognized the Telford cart and loaded the milled grain. George, being aggravated, waited until Monday and promptly returned the grain to the miller, "wanting no part of the sabbath-breaking grist."[389] The second event that demonstrates George's piety, or perhaps pettiness, was on another Sunday while he was traveling to church. On his path, he saw a neighbor exit the home, split a log into two pieces and return to his house with only one of the pieces. Witnessing this tormented George so much that he filed a formal complaint against the man for desecration of the Sabbath, though the local magistrates did not take the complaint seriously and dismissed it. This litigious background is common in witchcraft cases and oftentimes represents a history of neighbors' animosity toward the family of the accused leading up to an accusal event. Simply put, after numerous times of a family suing members of their small communities, the community is going to get upset at that family.

These tensions could not have come at a worse time, as the American Revolution was well underway, and the horrors of war surrounded their village. British general John Burgoyne was leading his campaign from Canada to Saratoga and had claimed victory over nearby Fort Edward, where he stationed his men. An Iroquois scouting party allied with the British had also been wreaking havoc on the settler community. Several men, women and children had been slaughtered in their homes, thus terrifying the families of Salem that they might be next. One of those murdered was Jane McCrea, whose death formed a rallying cry for many local settlers to take up arms, join the fight and eventually help overtake Burgoyne's army.[390] However, fearing for their lives, several families, including the Telfords, sought protection at Fort Edward under British general Burgoyne so that they wouldn't be murdered in their own homes. Unfortunately, the Telfords would have to answer for this action later on, charged "for going to the enemy,"[391] and prove their loyalty to the Patriots. Even though they were later vouched for by militia officer Captain John McKellop, community resentment toward the Telfords persisted.[392]

In 1777, tensions were high among the townsfolk of Salem, and people were certainly overwhelmed with the uncertainty of their futures. Amid this, Salem resident Archy Livingston discovered that the milk he received from his cows was unable to be churned into butter. Perplexed, Archy decided to visit a local fortune teller named Joel Dibble, a miscreant who was staying in the home where the Telfords first sheltered on their arrival in 1772. Dibble offered his services as a clairvoyant tradesman, shuffling and cutting a deck of cards in a performance of cartomancy,[393] to discover the cause of poor Archy Livingston's butter problem. The answer couldn't be any clearer to Joel Dibble—it was witchcraft. But who could this cruel witch be? A foe? a neighbor? The cards could not reveal any specific names to Joel Dibble but did describe the appearance of the culprit. It was a short and thick woman with black hair who had a red-haired daughter. Conveniently, this description matched one person in town, Margaret Telford.

Archy Livingston wasted no time alerting the community that Margaret Telford was a witch. Archy's father-in-law tried to stop him from spreading such inflammatory gossip, but it was of no use. The community of Salem, already on edge from the ongoing war, now had a threat from the supernatural to address. Magistrates during this period were more cautious to try cases involving witchcraft considering the new legal sentiments on the matter following the British Witchcraft Act of 1735. There was no formal trial, but since the Livingstons and Telfords were both members of Reverend Clark's congregation, it was decided best that Clark investigate the matter. Clark interviewed witnesses, some of whom spoke in support of Margaret.[394] The investigation soon turned to the cartomancer Joel Dibble. Dibble argued that he had paid to learn this form of fortune-telling in French Canada. This argument is important. Recall the details of seventeenth-century witchcraft prosecution: the dark and detestable arts practiced by suspected witches are only prosecutable if there is evidence that the suspected witch learned or gained their powers from an explicit deal with the devil. Since Dibble proclaimed he paid to learn these skills from an unknown source in French Canada, it precluded him from being accused of witchcraft himself. He further argued that the rules of cartomancy prevented him from making exact or detailed statements (in other words, naming specific individuals). This ended the investigation,

Telford family tombstones at the Revolutionary War Cemetery in Salem, New York. *Photograph by author.*

as there was nothing definable to charge against Margaret Telford—if anything, it was speculation at best. Reverend Clark moved away shortly after this event, and although the matter was irrelevant to local authorities, the issue felt unresolved to the Salem community members.[395] The Telfords continued to be ostracized from the community. This may well have been from the witchcraft accusation, George Telford's litigious proclivities or even their decision to seek temporary refugee within a British fort, which their neighbors rallied to defeat. Whatever the cause, the Telfords endured the brunt of all the community gossip. Their own son John, after becoming engaged to Sarah Rowan, became a target with many of Sarah's friends and relatives opposed to the relationship.[396] Margaret and her husband, George, lived out the remainder of their lives in Salem; Margaret died at seventy-six years old on September 15, 1807, and George followed her a few years later at eighty-four years old on July 23, 1813. They are both buried in the Revolutionary War Cemetery in Salem, Washington County, New York. However, George's name is spelled "George Telford," while Margaret is spelled "Tilford." And as the notable witchcraft historian John Demos would say, the Telfords' chapter comes to a close, and Margaret and George exit at stage left.

24

UNNAMED WOMAN NO. 3

In Cornplanter's village lived an old woman who, in the past, was suspected of being a witch, known for poisoning the families of her enemies. Cornplanter's daughter died under mysterious circumstances, and witchcraft was suspected. Cornplanter had to act fast to destroy the source of bewitchment now that an infant in his village was also threatened by similar symptoms that his late daughter had experienced. He ordered three of his sons to locate and execute the old woman. On June 13, 1799, the three men found the old woman working in the fields and slashed her throat.[397] No further information has been found to indicate if the infant recovered or perished following the murder.

25

NANCY JUSON

Nancy Juson's story is a rather short account and actually may be more fiction than fact. The only record of Nancy Juson's accusal comes from a historical reference book that provides the place name history of Staten Island.[398] The entry reads as follows:

Lambert's Lane leads from the Stone Road to Watchogue and is named on most maps of the Island. It was called after Lambert Merill, a carpenter by trade, whose housekeeper, Nancy Juson, according to the firm belief of the neighbors, was a veritable witch. A wagon load of hay was passing along the lane, and when opposite the Merill house was beset by unaccountable difficulties and directly overturned. The team following passed unharmed with its load, and Nancy declared that it was driven by a praying man over whom she could cast no spell. On one occasion Merill, while working in his shop, desired a mallet that was upstairs. Soon he heard it bump, bumping down the steps, and directly it shoved open the door and lay by his side. He did not want it then and so threw it upstairs, but directly it came bumping, bumping down the steps as before. Once more he threw it aloft, and when it persistently returned for the third time, he seized an axe and cut off its handle. The next day the witch had a sore leg.[399]

26

THE EIGHTEENTH CENTURY REVISITED

I t is clear that the belief in witchcraft persisted into the eighteenth century. However, the legal prosecution of witchcraft occurs only once during this century in a relatively isolated area on Long Island, namely, the Mary Newton case, in 1735—the year Britain passed its new Witchcraft Act. Unfortunately, the primary source documents from the Newton case contain very little information on the proceedings of this event, and we can only speculate, founded in the event's contemporary context, as to the details and motivations of the accusation. The Telford accusation made local magistrates uneasy, so this case was investigated by the community's religious leader instead of any legal authority. These two cases mark the only detailed descriptions we have of Euro-American communities casting blame for unfortunate circumstances on supernatural causes. Further, these two cases, similar to the last century, did not result in execution but rather acquittal of the individuals accused. However, we could be fairly certain these individuals did not escape the gossip that follows events such as these and likely lived the remainder of their lives haunted by whispers. Staten Island communities also developed their own anxieties and fears of witches during this century, though the lack of historical data makes it hard to discern whether these retellings happened or are regional folklore. However, it does seem plausible that the tale of Aunty Greenleaf is nothing more than folklore developed from Elizabeth Greenleaf's name (the first female pharmacist) and combined with therianthropic folklore as old as Ancient Greece, though adapted to fit within eighteenth-century Long Island contexts. Witchcraft among Native American communities is a bit more unforgiving, with higher instances of executing the accused—at least from the perspective of eighteenth-century European observers recording the events. It is understood that witchcraft fears and anxieties greatly affected Haudenosaunee communities, particularly the Seneca, at the turn of the nineteenth century. A more comprehensive discussion of these events can be found in Matthew Dennis's book *Seneca Possessed* (2012). Lastly, it is important to close this century off by underscoring that the victims of these horrible events were not just characters in this book but real people. The events that led to their accusation, and in some cases execution, were largely the result of a community's fears and anxieties getting the better hold of people's senses. Violent and politically charged environments often played a large role in these events. The particularities of each case are crucial for understanding why people not only believed in witchcraft but were willing to hurt their neighbors over this belief as well.

CONCLUSION

Whats important to understand is that witchcraft was not a superstition for people in the seventeenth and eighteenth centuries. It was as real as contracting a virus; it could do you harm, it could harm others and there were certain remedies to protect against it and prevent it from spreading. This connection between witchcraft and contagious diseases have been noted before in anthropological studies of this subject[400] and is a fascinating comparison. After all, many of the accused individuals in this book had some connection between the spread of disease and the accusations against them. Germ theory, or the spread of disease through microorganisms, was a conceptual thought just in its infancy during the seventeenth and eighteenth centuries. Our current understandings of epidemiology and public health were not yet realized, and witchcraft was still on par with viruses, all being attributed to the "wonders of the invisible world." However, as we have seen historically, stress from rapidly changing cultural and political landscapes also played a large role in creating atmospheres where community anxieties heightened, and neighbors became malicious strangers. The social environment of the seventeenth century was so precarious that strict order and conservative use of resources were demanded of every settler to maintain a balance. When that balance was disturbed then communities rushed to return to the status quo, largely through scapegoating. The association of unfortunate events to witchcraft was an easy way to explain disorder and personify this disorder by attributing it to an individual(s). Lastly, as you have now read, gossip was

Five silhouetted figures by Barbara Anne Townshend (1815). *Wellcome Collection*.

at the heart of witchcraft accusations. For most, this gossip was inescapable, even long after the witchcraft accusation event occurred.

The tragedy of witchcraft history is that for most accounts and testimonies, the victim is almost universally centered and we learn little about the lives of the accusers. What motivations did these community members have when accusing their neighbors of witchcraft? Often it is the gossip among accusers that spirals into formal accusations and legal proceedings, with sometimes numerous witnesses testifying about the habits and livelihood of an individual accused of witchcraft. Once you are in a position like this, the targeted individual everyone is ganging up on, it is very hard to flip the script and interrogate, or challenge, the credibility and innocence of the accusers. Even today, relying on extant primary source records, we can really only observe the individual accused of witchcraft and find great difficulty turning the spotlight on the accusers, at least when only consulting historical records. These accounts do offer insight on the struggles of being a woman in Puritan society. Our understandings of female agency and perspectives in the colonial period of American history would be more difficult to discern were it not for witchcraft trial accounts or any legal matter that was written down when it occurred. A crime as serious as witchcraft often prompted courts to transcribe these events and details.

It's incredibly difficult for us to understand and comprehend the social and natural world our ancestors lived in during the seventeenth and eighteenth centuries. Archaeologists and historians spend lifetimes attempting to understand and communicate certain aspects of life and types of human behavior through a critical analysis of historical texts and artifacts. I strongly encourage you to not only read more about the complexities and entanglements of early American settler-colonialism but also visit your local historical society and museums. This book, or any book really, can only bring you to the door and help guide your understanding of the past. Once you finish reading this book, you need to stand up, walk outside and experience these places and landscapes for yourself and make your own memories and experiences. I highly encourage you to participate in the history and heritage resources and events in your community. Go talk to your local town historian, visit the local historical society and museums, participate in your community's festivals and celebrations and not just from behind social media, but physically present. We are not as disconnected from the past as you would think. The consequences and legacies of the past are present all around us and form the way we currently view our world. Engage with it. Engage with history.

Witchcraft histories, particularly here in New York, form such an interesting aspect of our past. The places and landscapes mentioned here are still accessible today. You can go visit where these communities once stood. Most of these individuals were real, and even though these historical accounts may have read like fictional stories, you can go visit their old stomping grounds today.

Lastly, New York is different from any other state's history when it comes to witchcraft. When an individual was targeted as a witch, be it in a New York community or a neighboring colony, that individual(s) was offered legal protection and a safe haven from those who would see them senselessly killed. New York has a storied tradition of offering aid to those who had nowhere to turn, not only for those arriving from other colonies but also those arriving from different countries. Echoing are the words of Emma Lazarus, whose poem *The New Colossus* (1883) sits beneath the beckoning Statue of Liberty in New York Harbor, "*Send these, the homeless, tempest-tost to me, I lift my lamp beside the golden door.*"

NOTES

Introduction

1. Evans-Pritchard, *Witchcraft, Oracles and Magic.*
2. Moyer, *Detestable and Wicked Arts*, 53.
3. Augé, "Embedded Implication of Cultural Worldviews."
4. Ray, *Satan and Salem*, 198; Norton, *In the Devil's Snare.*
5. Ray, *Satan and Salem*, 201; Hansen, "Metamorphosis of Tituba."
6. Gellman, *Emancipating New York*, 153.
7. Upham, *Salem Witchcraft*, 437.
8 McMillan, "Black Magic," 106
9. Ibid.
10. Ibid.
11. Rosaldo, "Women, Culture, and Society," 31.
12. The first witchcraft museum in the United States was called the Buckland Museum of Witchcraft and Magick and was located at 6 First Avenue, Bay Shore, New York. This museum was in operation between 1966 and 1973. Raymond Buckland learned modern forms of witchcraft from Gerald Gardner (founder of Wicca) while visiting him in England and brought this form of spiritualism to the United States; "LI Museum Has School for Stellar Study," *Daily News*, January 9, 1972; www.bucklandmuseum.org/about-the-museum.

1. Introduction to the Seventeenth Century

13. Porterfield, "Witchcraft and Colonization."
14. Public decree.
15. Latin: "desiring with supreme ardor."

16. Darst, "Witchcraft in Spain."
17. Latin: "Hammer of the Witches"
18. Darst "Witchcraft in Spain."
19. Thurston, *Witch, Wicce, Mother Goose.*
20. "Demonology."
21. Porterfield, "Witchcraft and Colonization," 109–10.
22. Ibid., 109.
23. See Ankarloo, Clark and Monter, *Witchcraft and Magic in Europe*, 80–81.
24. Hedges, Pelletreau and Foster, *First Book of Records*, 18.
25. Old French: "Court of Sessions."
26. Old French: "To hear and determine."
27. Burr, "Witchcraft in New York," 46n2.
28. Griswold Van Rensselaer, *History of the City of New York*, 203.
29. Skinner, *Myths and Legends.*
30. Ibid.

2. The Jesuit Sorcerers:
Réne Goupil and Father Isaac Jogues and John de Lalande

31. Translates to "People of the Longhouse."
32. Engelbrecht, "Iroquois."
33. Huron: Ihonatiria.
34. Thwaites, *Jesuit Relations*, 42; Scott, *Isaac Jogues.*
35. Same as Ihonatiria.
36. A lay missionary is a servant of the Jesuit priests tasked with manual labor in service of the church.
37. Scott, *Isaac Jogues.*
38. Thwaites, *Jesuit Relations*, 28:125.
39. Onion, "Corn in the Culture," 62.
40. Thwaites, *Jesuit Relations*, 25:109
41. Cleaving the skull of a criminal was the prescribed method of execution for an accused within Native Americans cultures.
42. Thwaites, *Jesuit Relations*, 25:51; 28:133–36.
43. Ibid., 25:53.
44. Ibid., 25:57.

3. The Long Island Sachems: Sachem Poggatacut and Wyandanch's Agent

45. A sachem (anglicized eastern Algonquian) is a Native American chief of a tribe.
46. Pulsipher, *Records of the Colony*, 9:167.
47. Ales, "History of the Indians," 23; Strong, "Wyandanch"; De Forest, *History of the Indians*, 237–38; Thatcher, *Indian Biography.*
48. Jeremy Dennis, jeremynative.com; Siminoff, *Crossing the Sound*, 74.
49. Strong, "Wyandanch."

50. jeremynative.com; Siminoff, *Crossing the Sound*, 172; *History of Suffolk County*, 19.
51. Ceci, "Locational Analysis."
52. Strong, "Wyandanch."
53. Strong, "Thirteen Tribes of Long Island."
54. Occum, "Account of the Montauk Indians."
55. Ales, "History of the Indians," 7; Occum, "Account of the Montauk Indians," 109.
56. Ales, "History of the Indians," 8.
57. Ibid.; Occum, "Account of the Montauk Indians," 109.
58. Stone "Rites and Customs," 261.
59. Strong, "Wyandanch."
60. Ibid.
61. Ibid.
62. Ales, "History of the Indians," 23n27; Pulsipher, *Records of the Colony*, 9:167.
63. Pulsipher, *Records of the Colony*, 9:167.
64. Wampum was a currency used by both Native Americans and early European settlers and was made from carved whelk, clamshell or conch.
65. Ales, "History of the Indians," 23.
66. Strong, "Wyandanch"; Pulsipher, *Records of the Colony*, 10:169.
67. Strong, "Wyandanch."
68. Gardiner, *Chronicles of the Town of Easthampton*, 34.
69. jeremynative.com; Stone, "Rites and Customs," 229; Ales, "History of the Indians," 25.
70. jeremynative.com.

4. Cornelis Melyn (Moolyn)

71. "Betrothal Certificate of Cornelis Melijin & Jannetie Ariaenss," http://dgmweb.net/Resources/BMD/Mar-MelynCornelis-JannekenAdriaens.html.
72. "Patent. Cornelis Melyn."
73. Shorto, *Island at the Center of the World*, 114.
74. Ibid., 123,
75. Rine "Intercultural Contact," 65
76. Ibid.; Corwin, *Ecclesiastical Records*, 1:303.
77. Rine, "Intercultural Contact," 47.
78. Gehring, *New York Historical Manuscripts*, 5:225n90.
79. Ibid., 5:97.
80. Haefeli, "Dutch New York," 283.
81. Ibid., 284.

5. Goodwife Elizabeth Garlick

82. Orion, *It Were As Well*, 21,87; Demos, *Entertaining Satan*, 233, 470.
83. Demos, *Entertaining Satan*, 71; Orion, *It Were As Well*, 87. Demos consulted *Records and Files of the Quarterly Courts of Essex County Massachusetts*, vol 1:45, 57, 79, and also *New England and Genealogical Register*, 93:162–70.

84. Orion, *It Were As Well*, 7; Demos, *Entertaining Satan*, 233n50, 470.
85. Orion, *It Were As Well*, 7.
86. Ibid., 19; Hedges, *Records of the Town of East Hampton*.
87. A witch's familiar was believed to be a supernatural or demonic entity that assisted witches in their practice of magic.
88. Culpepper, *Complete Herbal*; Hildegard, *Healing Plants*.
89. Culpepper *Complete Herbal*.
90. Hildegard, *Healing Plants*.
91. Foster and Hobbs, *Field Guide*, 226.
92. Ibid., 236–39; Stansbury, *Herbal Formularies*, 48.
93. Herrick, *Iroquois Medical Botany*, 145–46.
94. Orion, *It Were As Well*, 25.
95. Ibid., 23
96. Ibid., 24.
97. Ibid., 7.
98. Ibid., 32.
99. Ibid., 32–33
100. Ibid., 37; Hedges, *Records of the Town of East Hampton*, 135.
101. Orion, *It Were As Well*, 37.
102. Hedges, *Records of the Town of East Hampton*, 140.
103. Records of the particular court of Connecticut, 1639–1663, Hartford, Connecticut.
104. Orion, *It Were As Well*, 39.
105. Ibid., 43
106. Ibid., 60n62, 91–92.
107. Gardiner, *History of the Pequot War*, 9.
108. Orion, *It Were As Well*, 59
109. Ibid., 60
110. Ibid., 44n41, 90.
111. Ibid., 45.
112. Ibid., 46; see "Winthrop Jr., John," in Trumbull, *Public Records of the Colony*, 572–73n33.
113. Orion, *It Were As Well*, 46, 61.
114. Ibid., 65.
115. Ibid., 66; Hedges, *Records of the Town of East Hampton*, 421.

6. Mary Wright Andrews

116. Drake, "Witchcraft in the American Colonies," 707; Lyon, "Witchcraft in New York," 273.
117. Thompson, *History of Long Island*, 270.
118. Hall, "The Puritans," 12.
119. Porterfield, *Female Piety*, 20.
120. Mack, *Visionary Women*.

121. Rogers, *Mary Dyer of Rhode Island*, 59

122. Sewel, *History of the Rise*, 354; Besse, *Collection of the Sufferings*, 224.

123. Hutchinson, *History of Massachusetts*, 186–87.

124. Perrine, *Wright Family*, 49

125. Ibid.; Sewel, *History of the Rise*, 417; Besse, *Collection of the Sufferings*, 225

126. Perrine, *Wright Family*, 50.

127. Perrine, *Wright Family*, 50; Sewel, *History of the Rise*, 423. To "drink a dram" is an old phrases meaning "drinking whiskey," and a dram"is about one mouthful of alcohol.

128. Perrine, *Wright Family*, 52.

129. Ibid., 53–54; Hill, *History of the Old South Church*,1:219; Besse, *Collection of the Sufferings*, 263.

130. Perrine, *Wright Family*, 54; Besse, *Collection of the Sufferings*, 264.

131. Perrine, *Wright Family*, 55.

132. Ibid., 50–51.

133. Ibid., 57.

7. The Hartford Hysteria: Judith Varleth Bayard and Goodwife Ayres

134. Wyllys Papers BUL. The Wyllys Papers are housed in two separate repositories: the Connecticut State Public Library (CTSL) Collection and the Brown University Library (BUL) Collection.

135. Spencer-Molloy, "Science Casts New Light"; Steiner, *History of Medicine*.

136. Spencer-Molloy, "Science Casts New Light"; Steiner, *History of Medicine*; "First Postmortem." Retrospective medical diagnoses of individuals from historical documents should always be dealt with a degree of skepticism.

137. Walker, *History of the First Church*, 176–77; Mather, *Magnalia Christi Americana*, 448–49.

138. Taylor, *Witchcraft Delusion*, 96.

139. For original text, see Taylor, *Witchcraft Delusion*, 99–100.

140. Letter from Petrus Stuyvesant to Hartford, in Brodhead, *Documents Relating to the Colonial History*, 14:518.

141. Haefeli, "Dutch New York."

142. Brodhead, *Documents Relating to the Colonial History*, 13:281.

8. Mary Hall and Ralph Hall

143. Barstow, *Setauket, Alias Brookhaven*, 197; Strong, "Book Review of Belle Barstow," 240.

144. Barstow, *Setauket, Alias Brookhaven*, 196.

145. Ibid., 387; Weeks, *Brookhaven Town Records*, 125

146. Burr, "Witchcraft in New York," 44; Moyer, *Detestable and Wicked Arts*, 1; *Long Island Courant*, 1965.

147. Patchogue, *Records of the Town of Brookhaven*, 38.
148. This is admittedly speculation, as there is no definitive recorded relationship between George Wood and the Halls.
149. Barstow, *Setauket, Alias Brookhaven*, 199.
150. Ibid.
151. Clark, "Rhode Island Woods," 131.
152. Barstow, *Setauket, Alias Brookhaven*, 195n.
153. Strong, "Book Review of Belle Barstow," 240.
154. O'Callaghan, *Colonial History*, 4:86.
155. Thomas Baker's home is still standing today as a bed-and-breakfast in East Hampton, New York, known as the Baker House 1650. A great way of connecting to this history is not only visiting this site but also spending a night in one of the rooms. This B&B is located at 181 Main Street.
156. Likely Sheriff William Hallet; Burr, "Witchcraft in New York," 44.
157. O'Callaghan, *Colonial History*. 4:85.
158. Ibid., 86.
159. Moyer, *Detestable and Wicked Arts*, 3.
160. O'Callaghan, *Colonial History*, 4:86.
161. Weeks, *Brookhaven Town Records*, 100.
162. Tooker, *Indian Place Names*, 151.
163. Ibid., 152.
164. Thompson, *History of Long Island*, 321.
165. Weeks, *Brookhaven Town Records*, 100.
166. Innes, "Earliest Records of Brookhaven," 438.
167. Weeks, *Brookhaven Town Records*, 100; Barstow, *Setauket, Alias Brookhaven*, 387.
168. Hall, "High Freshets and Low-Lying Farms," 208n44.
169. Weeks, *Brookhaven Town Records*, 93.
170. Ibid., 125.
171. Moyer, *Detestable and Wicked Arts*, 3; O'Callaghan, *Colonial History*, 2:527.

9. Katherine Harrison

172. Jenkins, *Story of the Bronx*, 58.
173. Based off the incomplete historical record of the lives of women in the seventeenth century.
174. Demos, *Entertaining Satan*, 356.
175. Ibid., 338.
176. Ibid.
177. Ibid.
178. Ibid., 338n11–98; Deposition of Thomas Waples; Wyllys Papers CTSL.
179. Connell, "Great or Notorious Liar," 5–6.
180. Demos, *Entertaining Satan*, 357:105.
181. Ibid., 170, 359n116.
182. Burr, "Witchcraft in New York," 48n2; Demos, *Entertaining Satan*, 359.

183. Demos, *Entertaining Satan*, 341, 358.

184. Ibid., 358.

185. Ibid., 358n108.

186. Ibid., 64; deposition by "the wife of Jacob Johnson" in the trial of Katherine Harrison, Wyllys Papers, W–16.

187. Brader, "Oils, Ointments and Plasters."

188. Ibid.

189. This division of four witchcraft-practice categories was adopted from Walter Woodward's work exploring the testimonies against Harrison, but through the form of a school lesson plan designed to guide students through the legal proceedings of witchcraft trials during this time period. See Woodward, "Trial of Katherine Harrison," 38.

190. Wyllys Papers BUL/CTSL.

191. Wyllys Papers BUL.

192. Wyllys Papers CTSL.

193. Wyllys Papers CTSL.

194. Wyllys Papers CTSL.

195. Wyllys Papers BUL.

196. Wyllys Papers CTSL, W-7.

197. Wyllys Papers CTSL.

198. Wyllys Papers BUL.

199. Connell, "Great or Notorious Liar," 14.

200. Wyllys Papers BUL.

201. Connell, "Great or Notorious Liar," 15n58; Records of the Particular Court of Connecticut, 124–25.

202. Connell, "Great or Notorious Liar," 15.

203. Ibid., 16.

204. There can be much more said about James Wakley, but for further information on him, see Demos, *Entertaining Satan*.

205. Wyllys Papers BUL.

206. Wyllys Papers CTSL.

207. Wyllys Papers CTSL.

208. Wyllys Papers CTSL 6–17.

209. Wyllys Papers BUL.

210. Wyllys Papers BUL.

211. Karlsen, *Devil in the Shape*, 86.

212. Wyllys Papers BUL.

213. Connell, "Great or Notorious Liar," 10.

214. Woodward, *Prospero's America*, 238.

215. Connell, "Great or Notorious Liar," 18.

216. Ibid., 17.

217. Ibid., 11; see also *The Answers of Some Ministers to the Questions Propounded to Them by the Honored Magistrates* in Wyllys Papers BUL: Supplement, Document W–18.

218. Connell, "Great or Notorious Liar," 10.

219. Wyllys Papers BUL; Woodward, "Trial of Katherine Harrison."

220. Wyllys Papers, BUL; Woodward, "Trial of Katherine Harrison."
221. Connell, "Great or Notorious Liar," 13; Reis, *Damned Women*, 75.
222. Connell, "Great or Notorious Liar," 13.
223. Wyllys Papers BUL; Woodward, "Trial of Katherine Harrison."
224. Connell, "Great or Notorious Liar," 13.
225. Ibid.
226. Demos, *Entertaining Satan*, 363.
227. In 1670, the Kings Highway was laid out along the Connecticut River; see Goodwin, *East Hartford*, 68.
228. Riddell, "Witchcraft in Old New York," 252.
229. O'Callaghan, "Trial for Witchcraft," 87.
230. Ibid.
231. Van Laer, *Minutes of the Court of Albany*, 195–98.
232. O'Callaghan, "Trial for Witchcraft," 87.
233. Ibid., 88.
234. Riddell "Witchcraft in Old New York," 255.
235. Ibid.
236. Demos, *Entertaining Satan*, 363, 517n140; *Minutes of the Executive Council*, 2:393–95; Fernow, *Records of New Amsterdam*, 6:302, 306
237. Karlsen, *Devil in the Shape*, 89.
238. Demos, *Entertaining Satan*, 363; Drake, *Annals of Witchcraft*, 133–34; Levermore, "Witchcraft in Connecticut," 812.

10. Maes Cornelis Van Bloemendaal / Van Buren

239. Van Laer, *Minutes of the Court of Albany*, 595.
240. Peckham and Van Buren, *History of Cornelis Maessen Van Buren*, 219.
241. Ostrander and Ostrander, *Ostrander*, 244
242. Van Laer, *Minutes of the Court of Albany*.
243. Ibid., 195–98.
244. Piwonka, "Lutheran Presence in New Netherland," 3.
245. Located at 39 Fifth Street, Athens, NY 12015.
246. Van Laer, *Minutes of the Court of Albany*, 523.
247. Ibid., 542.
248. Haefeli, "Dutch New York."
249. Burr, "Witchcraft in New York."
250. An apt comparison would be the popularity of paranormal investigators in the present day and the belief in demonic hauntings of a historic property, even though academic scholars largely discount supernatural causes for strange and unusual occurrences attributed to the invisible. The point being, even though intellectuals and scholars are skeptical in their discussion about certain belief systems and the credibility of supernatural forces, the general public maintain these beliefs and fascinations in the potential harm from the supernatural.
251. Wheeler, "Apotropaic Building Practices."

11. Hannah Horton Hildreth Bower Travally (Trevalle)

252. Pelletreau, *Abstracts of Wills*; Dinan, *In Search of Barnabas*, 175.
253. For more about Barnabas Horton, see Dinan, *In Search of Barnabas*.
254. Dinan, *In Search of Barnabas*, 175; McLaurin, *Descendants of Barnabas Horton*, 174–78.
255. Dinan, *In Search of Barnabas*, 279.
256. Howell, *Early History of Southampton*, 156.
257. Dinan, *In Search of Barnabas*.
258. Howell, *Early History of Southampton*, 33; Sheppard, "Origin of the Bowers," 211.
259. Pelletreau, *Abstracts of Wills*, 22.
260. A cooper is a barrel maker.
261. Dinan, *In Search of Barnabas*, 280.
262. Pelletreau, *Abstracts of Wills*, 110.
263. Howell, *Early History of Southampton*, 95–96.
264. Dinan, *In Search of Barnabas*, 279.

12. Goodwife Miller

265. Ranlet, "Safe Haven for Witches?" 43.
266. Godbeer, *Escaping Salem*, 21.
267. Ibid.
268. Ibid., 33
269. Ibid., 15.
270. Ibid., 15–16.
271. Taylor, *Witchcraft Delusion*.
272. Godbeer, *Escaping Salem*, 16–17.
273. Ibid., 16.
274. Ibid., 17.
275. Ibid., 18.
276. Ibid., 19.
277. Ibid., 152.
278. Ibid., 20.
279. Ibid.
280. Ibid., 25.
281. Ibid., 26.
282. Ibid., 27.
283. Ibid.
284. Ibid.
285. Ibid., 28.
286. Le Beau, *Story of the Salem Witch*, 104.
287. Godbeer, *Escaping Salem*, 30.
288. Ibid.
289. Ibid., 37.
290. Ibid.

291. Ranlet, "Safe Haven for Witches?" 44; Godbeer, *Escaping Salem*, 57–58.

292. Ranlet, "Safe Haven for Witches?" 44.

293. Ibid.

294. Ibid.

295. Godbeer, *Escaping Salem*, 58.

296. Ibid., 59.

297. Ibid., 61.

298. Ranlet, "Safe Haven for Witches?" 44.

299. Hall, *Witch-Hunting in Seventeenth-Century*, 332.

300. Ranlet, "Safe Haven for Witches?" 44.

301. Ibid.

302. Godbeer, *Escaping Salem*, 140.

13. The Salem Refugees

303. In 1998, archaeological excavations on Governors Island, New York City, by the Public Archaeology Laboratory Inc. uncovered the remains of a wind-powered sawmill from 1625. The investigation led researchers to discover one of the owners of this sawmill was Edward Bishop, who later moved to Salem, Massachusetts. His second or third wife, Bridget Bishop, was one of the nineteen executed for witchcraft (Huey, "Archaeology of 17th-Century New Netherland," 106).

304. Haefeli, "Dutch New York," 278.

305. Ranlet, "Safe Haven for Witches?," 50.

306. Ibid., 53.

307. Belknap, "Philip English, Commerce Builder," 20.

308. Le Beau, *Story of the Salem Witch*, 101.

309. Ibid.

310. "Samplers (left) Made by Mary Hollingworth, Married 1 July, 1676, to Philip English. [...] Also (right) Made by Eunice Bowditch, aged 11, 1 July, 1718," New York Public Library Digital Collections, https://digitalcollections.nypl.org/items/510d47d9-5119-a3d9-e040-e00a18064a99.

311. Belknap, "Philip English, Commerce Builder," 20.

312. Bernau, "Ancestry of Philip English," 40–41.

313. Belknap, "Philip English, Commerce Builder," 20.

314. Ibid.

315. Le Beau, *Story of the Salem Witch*, 102.

316. Ibid., 103.

317. Ibid., 102.

318. Belknap, "Philip English, Commerce Builder," 22; Drake, "Book of New England Legends," 176; Le Beau, *Story of the Salem Witch*, 100.

319. Le Beau, *Story of the Salem Witch*, 103.

320. Ibid.

321. Ibid., 104.

322. Belknap, "Philip English, Commerce Builder," 22; Le Beau, *Story of the Salem Witch*, 104.

323. Belknap, "Philip English, Commerce Builder," 22; Le Beau, *Story of the Salem Witch*, 104; Skinner, *Myths and Legends*.
324. Calef, *More Wonders of the Invisible*, 108.
325. Skinner, *Myths and Legends*.
326. Belknap, "Philip English, Commerce Builder," 23; Le Beau, *Story of the Salem Witch*, 105.
327. Weiser-Alexander, "Witches of Massachusetts"; Le Beau, *Story of the Salem Witch*, 119.
328. Calef, *More Wonders of the Invisible*, 95–98.

14. Winifred King Benham and Daughter

329. Leclerc and Simons, "Origin of Accused Witch," 162; Karlsen, *Devil in the Shape*, 44.
330. Leclerc and Simons, "Origin of Accused Witch," 168.
331. Gillespie, *Historic Record of Meriden*, 255.
332. Ibid.
333. Leclerc and Simons, "Origin of Accused Witch," 163.
334. Ibid.
335. Gillespie, *Historic Record of Meriden*, 255.
336. Ibid.
337. Ibid.
338. Ibid., 256.
339. Ibid.
340. Ibid.
341. Ibid., 267.
342. Ibid., 257.
343. Leclerc and Simons, "Origin of Accused Witch," 164; "Connecticut Witches," 958; Calef, *More Wonders of the Invisible*, 142–43.
344. Leclerc and Simons, "Origin of Accused Witch," 171; "Connecticut Witches," 957.
345. "Connecticut Witches," 957.
346. Gillespie, *Historic Record of Meriden*, 258.
347. Ibid.
348. Ibid.
349. Ibid., 258–59
350. Calef, *More Wonders of the Invisible*, 142–43.
351. Leclerc and Simons, "Origin of Accused Witch," 168.
352. "Connecticut Witches," 958.
353. Ibid.
354. Ibid.
355. Leclerc and Simons, "Origin of Accused Witch," 171; "Connecticut Witches," 958.
356. "Connecticut Witches," 958

16. Introduction to the Eighteenth Century

357. Davies, *Witchcraft, Magic and Culture*.

17. Unnamed Woman No. 1: Alleged Bewitcher of Aquendero's Son

358. Drake, *Annals of Witchcraft*, 208–10; see O'Callaghan, *Colonial History*, vol. 4, 689.
359. Crawford, "Security Regime Among Democracies," 364.

18. Unnamed Woman No. 2 (1710–1720)

360. Morris, *History of Staten Island*.
361. Ibid., 50.
362. Ibid., 49.
363. Ibid., 51.

19. Aunty Greenleaf

364. This year, 1727, is determined by Elizabeth Gooking Greenleaf. This was the year Greenleaf opened her apothecary shop in Boston. Although this does not relate to the first publication of the folkloric legend, it grounds the legend in the factual historical event.
365. Greenburg, *100 Wicked Little Witch Stories*; Schlosser, *Spooky New York*; Thompson, *Body, Boots, and Britches*.
366. Similar to Goody Garlick case.
367. Also similar to Goody Garlick.
368. Folklore scholars would recognize this literary trope as it dates back to the first century AD with *Satyricon* by Petronius, the oldest written account of a shape-shifter being injured in animal form and then discovered upon returning to human form and displaying injuries identical to those sustained to their beast form. See *Satyricon*, section 62.
369. Speck, "Shamanism," 294.
370. Bierhorst, *White Deer*.
371. Halsey, "Sketches from Local History," 156.
372. Another story of folklore concerns a Granny Mott in Rhode Island. See Bourgaize, "Supernatural Folklore of Rhode Island," 41–42.
373. Smith, *Myths of the Iroquois*, 73.

20. Buckinjehillish

374. Riddell, "Witchcraft in Old New York," 258; Seaver, *Narrative of the Life*, 170.

21. Mary Newton

375. First Minute Book, Town of Islip, 453.
376. Blinder, "Islip Once Investigated."
377. George Munkenbeck, personal communication with author, 2020; Blinder, "Islip Once Investigated."
378. Munkenbeck, personal communication; Blinder, "Islip Once Investigated."

22. Mary Jemison

379. What we know about Mary Jemison's story comes from a firsthand account in which Mary, at eighty years old, told her life story in great detail to a biographer who had intentionally sought her out to transcribe and preserve her life experiences. The interview was extensive and resulted in a book published a year after the interview. This brief retelling included here merely condenses and summarizes the book and the lived experiences of Mary Jemison, and it is highly advised to the reader that you find her original account, available free online in a number of different websites, and read the words as she spoke them. However, this text should be read with a degree of caution, as it is suspected that the transcriber, Seaver, inserted his own anti-Native sentiments and European essentialism in the biography's embellishments. Regardless, I have attempted to include certain excerpts here to convey her passion and memory.
380. Manetta, "Fort Loudoun."
381. Seaver, *Narrative of the Life*.
382. I have refrained from listing an expanded estimate of individuals accused/executed of witchcraft because this number is difficult to determine. However, *Seneca Possessed* by Matthew Dennis explores the Seneca Witch Trials in depth and should be consulted for further information.
383. Seaver, *Narrative of the Life*, 143–44.

23. Margaret Telford

384. This account is a retelling of John R. Henderson's scholarship on the Telford family genealogy; Salem, New York town history; and the Margaret Telford witchcraft case. For a more comprehensive discussion of this case, readers should consult Henderson's essay "The Witch of Salem, New York," published online at icyousee.org (2014).
385. Henderson, "Witch of Salem."
386. Ibid.
387. Ibid.
388. Ibid.
389. Ibid.
390. Wilson, *Life of Jane McCrea*.
391. Henderson, "Witch of Salem."

NOTES TO PAGES 166–173

392. Ibid.
393. Cartomancy is a form of fortune-telling in which a deck of playing cards is shuffled, dealt and interpreted in unique ways that vaguely answer the questions of those involved in the performance. This specific case presents interesting potential into cartomancy historical research, as not much is known about the ubiquity of the practice in eighteenth-century America, at least not until the rise of spiritualism in later centuries.
394. Henderson, "Witch of Salem."
395. Ibid.
396. Ibid.

24. Unnamed Woman No. 3

397. Dennis, *Seneca Possessed*, 96.

25. Nancy Juson

398. Davis, *Staten Island Names*, 61.
399. Ibid.

Conclusion

400. Douglas, "Witchcraft and Leprosy."

BIBLIOGRAPHY

Ales, Marion Fisher. "A History of the Indians on Montauk, Long Island." In *The History and Archaeology of the Montauk, Readings in Long Island Archaeology and Ethnohistory*, vol 3., edited by Gaynell Stone. 2nd ed. Stony Brook, NY: Suffolk County Archaeological Association and Nassau County Archaeological Committee, 1993.

Ankarloo, Bengt, Stuart Clark and William Monter. *Witchcraft and Magic in Europe: The Period of the Witch Trials*. 4th ed. London, UK: Athlone Press, 2002.

Augé, Cynthia Kay Riley. "Embedded Implication of Cultural Worldviews in the Use and Pattern of Magical Material Culture." *Historical Archaeology* 48, no. 3 (2014): 165–77.

———. "Silent Sentinels: Archaeology, Magic, and the Gendered Control of Domestic Boundaries in New England, 1620–1725." PhD dissertation, the University of Montana, 2013.

Barstow, Belle. *Setauket, Alias Brookhaven: The Birth of a Long Island Town with Chronological Records 1655–1679*. New York: Author-House, 2004.

Belknap, Henry W. "Philip English, Commerce Builder." In *Proceedings of the American Antiquarian Society* 41, no. 1 (1931): 17–24.

Bernau, Charles A. "Ancestry of Philip English, Seventeenth Century Merchant of Salem. Some Notes on the Family of L'Anglois, of Jersey." In *The Essex Institute Historical Collections*, vol. 75. Salem, MA: Newcomb and Gauss Company Printers, 1939.

Besse, Joesph. *A Collection of the Sufferings of the People Called Quakers for the Testimony of a Good Conscience*. Vol. 2. London: Luke Hinde Printer, 1753.

Bierhorst, John. *The White Deer and Other Stories Told by the Lenape*. New York: William Morrow, 1997.

Blanchard, David. "Who or What's a Witch? Iroquois Persons of Power." *American Indian Quarterly* 6, no. 3/4 (1982): 218–37.

Blinder, Rachelle. "Islip Once Investigated Accused Witch, Historian Says." *Newsday*, October 30, 2018.

Bourgaize, Eidola Jean. "Supernatural Folklore of Rhode Island." Master's thesis, University of Rhode Island, 1956.

Brader, Elisabeth. "Oils, Ointments and Plasters." *Early Modern Medicine Blog*, https://earlymodernmedicine.com.

Bradley, James W. "Onondaga and Empire: Iroquoian People in an Imperial Era." *New York State Museum Bulletin* 514 (2020).

Brodhead, John Romeyn. *Documents Relating to the Colonial History of the State of New York*. Vols. 13, 14. Edited by E.B. O'Callaghan. Albany, NY: Weed, Parsons and Company, 1883.

Burr, George Lincoln. "Witchcraft in New York, The Cases of Hall and Harrison." In *Narratives of the Witchcraft Cases 1648–1706*. New York: C. Scribner's Sons, 1914.

Burton, Paul Gibson. "Cornelis Melyn, Patroon of Staten Island and Some of His Descendants." *New York Genealogical and Biographical Record*, 1937.

Butler, Jon. "Magic, Astrology, and the Early American Religious Heritage, 1600–1760." *American Historical Review* 84, no. 2 (1979): 317–46.

Calef, Robert. *More Wonders of the Invisible World: Or, The Wonders of the Invisible World Displayed. In Five Parts*. Salem, MA: John D. and T.C. Cushing Jr., 1823.

Carlton, Charles. "The Widow's Tale: Male Myths and Female Reality in 16th and 17th Century England." *Albion* 10, no. 2 (1978): 118–29.

Carr, Lloyd G, and Carlos Westey. "Surviving Folktales and Herbal Lore Among the Shinnecock Indians of Long Island." *Journal of American Folklore* 58, no. 228 (1945): 113–23.

Ceci, Lynn. "Locational Analysis of Historic Algonquian Sites in Coastal New York: A Preliminary Study." Research Report. Proceedings of the Conference of Northeastern Archaeology. Department of Anthropology: University of Massachusetts-Amherst, 1980.

Clark, Bertha. "Rhode Island Woods on Long Island." *American Genealogist* 39 (1963): 131.

"Connecticut Witches." *American Genealogist* 4, no. 3 (1927): 951–58.

Connell, Liam. "'A Great or Notorious Liar': Katherine Harrison and Her Neighbours, Wethersfield, Connecticut, 1668–1670." *Eras* 12, no. 2 (2011).

Corwin, Edward T., ed. *Ecclesiastical Records of the State of New York*. Vol. 1. Albany: State of New York, 1901.

Crawford, Neta C. "A Security Regime Among Democracies: Cooperation Among Iroquois Nations." *International Organization* 48, no. 3 (1993): 345–85.

Culpepper, Nicholas. *Complete Herbal*. London: Arcturus Publishing Limited, 2020.

Darst, David H. "Witchcraft in Spain: The Testimony of Martín de Castañega's Treatise on Superstition and Witchcraft (1529)." *Proceedings of the American Philosophical Society* (1979): 298–322.

Davies, Owen. *Witchcraft, Magic and Culture, 1736–1951*. Manchester, UK: Manchester University Press, 1999.

Davis, Natalie Zemon. "Iroquois Women, European Women." In *Women, "Race" and Writing in the Early Modern Period*, edited by Margo Hendricks and Patricia Parker, 241–58. London: Routledge, 1994.

Davis, William Thompson, and Charles William Leng. *Staten Island Names: Ye Olde Names and Nicknames*. Natural Science Association, 1896.

De Forest, John William. *History of the Indians of Connecticut from the Earliest Known Period to 1850*. W.J. Hamersley, 1852.

Demos, John. "Underlying Themes in the Witchcraft of Seventeenth-Century New England." *American Historical Review* 75, no. 5 (1970): 1311–26.

Demos, John Putnam. *Entertaining Satan: Witchcraft and the Culture of Early New England*. New York: Oxford University Press, 2004.

Dennis, Matthew. "American Indians, Witchcraft, and Witch-Hunting." *OAH Magazine of History* 17, no. 4 (2003): 21–27.

———. "Patriarchy and the Witch-Hunting of Handsome Lake." In *Seneca Possessed: Indians, Witchcraft, and Power in the Early American Republic*, 81–116. Philadelphia: University of Pennsylvania Press, 2010.

Dennis, Matthew, and Elizabeth Reis. "3. Women as Witches, Witches as Women." In *Women in Early America*, 66–94. New York University Press, 2015.

Dinan, Jacqueline. *In Search of Barnabas Horton*. New York: Pynsleade Books, 2015.

Douglas, Mary. "Witchcraft and Leprosy: Two Strategies of Exclusion." *Man* 26, no. 4 (1991):723–36.

Drake, Frederick C. "Witchcraft in the American Colonies, 1647–62." *American Quarterly* 20, no. 4 (1968): 694–725.

Drake, Samuel Adams. *A Book of New England Legends and Folk Lore: In Prose and Poetry*. Boston: Little, Brown and Company, 1910.

Drake, Samuel G. *Annals of Witchcraft in New England and Elsewhere in the United States from Their First Settlement; Drawn Up from Unpublished and Other Well Authenticated Records of the Alleged Operations of Witches and Their Instigator, the Devil*. New York: Burt Franklin, 1869.

Dziuba, Andrzej Franciszek, et al. "Empire: The Rise and Demise of the British World Order and the Lessons for Global Power." *Łódzkie Studia Teologiczne* 16, no. 1 (2007): 285–88.

Engelbrecht, William. "The Iroquois: Archaeological Patterning on the Tribal Level." *World Archaeology* 6, no. 1 (June 1974): 52–65.

Evans-Pritchard, Edward E. "Witchcraft." *Africa* 8, no. 4 (1935): 417–22.

———. *Witchcraft, Oracles and Magic Among the Azande*. Vol. 12. Oxford, UK: Clarendon Press, 1937.

Fennell, Christopher C. "Conjuring Boundaries: Inferring Past Identities from Religious Artifacts." *International Journal of Historical Archaeology* 4, no. 4 (2000): 281–313.

Fernow, Berthold, ed. *The Records of New Amsterdam*. Vol. 6. New York, 1897.

"The First Postmortem Recorded in This County." *Journal of the American Medical Association* 21, no. 18 (1893): 661–62.

Foster, Steven, and Christopher Hobbs. *A Field Guide to Western Medicinal Plants and Herbs*. Boston: Houghton Mifflin Harcourt, 2002.

Gardiner, David. *Chronicles of the Town of Easthampton, County of Suffolk, New York*. Easthampton, NY: Bowne & Company, 1871.

Gardiner, Lion. *A History of the Pequot War: Or, A Relation of the War Between the Powerful Nation of Pequot Indians, Once Inhabiting the Coast of New-England, Westerly from Near Narraganset Bay and the English Inhabitants, in the Year 1638*. J. Harpel, 1860.

Gehring, Charles T., ed. *New York Historical Manuscripts: Dutch. Council Minutes, 1652–1654*. Vol. 5. Baltimore, MD: Genealogical Publishing Company Inc., 1983.

Gellman, David Nathaniel. *Emancipating New York: The Politics of Slavery and Freedom, 1777–1827*. Baton Rouge: Louisiana State University Press, 2006.

Gillespie, Charles Bancroft. *An Historic Record and Pictorial Description of the Town of Meriden, Connecticut and Men Who Have Made It*. Journal Publishing Company, 1906.

Godbeer, Richard. *Escaping Salem: The Other Witch Hunt of 1692*. New York: Oxford University Press, 2004.

Goodwin, Joseph O. *East Hartford: Its History and Traditions*. Hartford, CT: Press of the Case, Lockwood and Brainard Company, 1879.

Greenburg, Martin H. *100 Wicked Little Witch Stories*. New York: Barnes and Noble, 1995.

Griswold Van Rensselaer, Marianna. *History of the City of New York in the Seventeenth Century*. Vol. 1. New York: Macmillan Company, 1909.

Haake, Claudia B. "Appeals to Civilization and 'Customary Forest Diplomacy': Arguments against Removal in Letters Written by the Iroquois, 1830–1857." *Wicazo Sa Review* 30, no. 2 (2015): 100–128.

Haefeli, Evan. "Dutch New York and the Salem Witch Trials: Some New Evidence." In *Proceedings of the American Antiquarian Society* 110 (2003): 277–308.

Hall, David D. "The Puritans." In *The Puritans*. Princeton, NJ: Princeton University Press, 2019.

———. *Witch-Hunting in Seventeenth-Century New England: A Documentary History 1638–1693*. Durham, NC: Duke University Press, 2005.

Hall, Jason. "High Freshets and Low-Lying Farms: Property Law and St. John River Flooding in Colonial New Brunswick." *Dalhousie Law Journal* 39 (2016): 195.

Halsey, William Donaldson. *Sketches from Local History*. Bridgehampton, NY, 1935.

Hansen, Chadwick. "The Metamorphosis of Tituba, or Why American Intellectuals Can't Tell and Indian Witch from a Negro." *New England Quarterly* 47, no. 1 (1974): 3–12.

Harner, Michael J. "The Role of Hallucinogenic Plants in European Witchcraft." In *Hallucinogens and Shamanism*. New York: Oxford University Press, 1973.

Harring, Sidney L. "Red Lilac of the Cayugas: Traditional Indian Law and Culture Conflict in a Witchcraft Trial in Buffalo, New York, 1930." *New York History* 73, no. 1 (1992): 65.

Hayes, Katherine Frances Howlett. *Race Histories: Colonial Pluralism and the Production of History at the Sylvester Manor Site, Shelter Island, New York*. Berkeley: University of California Press, 2008.

Hedges, Henry Parsons. *Records of the Town of East Hampton (Feb 24, 1657–March 11, 1657)*. Vol. 1. Sag Harbor, NY: John H. Hart, Printer, 1897.

Hedges, Henry Parsons, William S. Pelletreau and Edward H. Foster. *The First Book of Records of the Town of Southampton with Other Ancient Documents of Historic Value*. Sag Harbor, NY: John H. Hunt Book and Job Printer, 1874.

Henderson, John R. "The Witch of Salem, New York." *ICYouSee* (blog), 2014. http://www.icyousee.org/witch.html.

Herrick, James W. *Iroquois Medical Botany*. Syracuse, NY: Syracuse University Press, 1995.

Hildegard of Bingens (1098–1179). *Healing Plants*. Beacon Press, 2001.

Hill, Frances. *A Delusion of Satan: The Full Story of the Salem Witch Trials*. Tantor eBooks, 2014.

Hill, Hamilton Andrews. *History of the Old South Church–Boston (1669–1884)*. 2 vols. Cambridge, MA: Houghton Mifflin and Company, 1890.

History of Suffolk County. New York: W.W. Munsell and Company, 1882.

Hoggard, Brian. *Magical House Protection: The Archaeology of Counter-Witchcraft*. New York: Berghahn Books, 2019.

Howell, George Rogers. *The Early History of Southampton, L.I. New York, with Genealogies*. New York: James Miller's Bookstore, 1866.

Huey, Paul R. "The Archaeology of 17th-Century New Netherland Since 1985: An Update." *Northeast Historical Archaeology* 34, no. 1 (2005): 6.

Hutchinson, Thomas. *The History of Massachusetts from the First Settlement Thereof in 1626, Until the Year 1750*. Vol. 1. 3rd ed. Salem, MA: Thomas C. Cushing Printer, 1795.

Innes, John H. "The Earliest Records of Brookhaven (Setauket) on Long Island." *New York History* 16, no. 4 (1935): 436–48.

Jenkins, Stephen. *The Story of the Bronx: From the Purchase Made by the Dutch from the Indians in 1639 to the Present Day*. New York: G.P. Putnam's Sons, 1912.

Karlsen, Carol. *The Devil in the Shape of a Woman: Witchcraft in Colonial New England*. New York: W.W. Norton and Company, 1987.

Le Beau, Bryan F. *The Story of the Salem Witch Trials*. 2nd ed. London: Routledge, 2016.

Leclerc, Michael, and D. Brenton Simons. "Origin of Accused Witch Mary (Williams)(King?) Hale of Boston and Her Brothers Hugh, John, and Possibly, Nathaniel Williams." *American Genealogist* 82, no. 3 (2007): 161–71.

Leone, Mark P., and Gladys-Marie Fry. "Conjuring in the Big House Kitchen: An Interpretation of African American Belief Systems Based on the Uses of Archaeology and Folklore Sources." *Journal of American Folklore* 112, no. 445 (1999): 372–403.

Levack, Brian P. *The Oxford Handbook of Witchcraft in Early Modern Europe and Colonial America*. New York: Oxford University Press, 2013.

Levermore, C.H. "Witchcraft in Connecticut." *New Englander* 44 (1885): 812.

Lolis, Thomas. "The City of Witches: James I, the Unholy Sabbath, and the Homosocial Refashioning of the Witches' Community." *Clio: A Journal of Literature, History, and the Philosophy of History* 37, no. 3 (2008).

Lucas, Michael T. "Empowered Objects: Material Expressions of Spiritual Beliefs in the Colonial Chesapeake Region." *Historical Archaeology* 48, no. 3 (2014): 106–24.

Lyon, John. "Witchcraft in New York." *New York Historical Society Collections* 2 (1869): 273–76.

Mack, Phyllis. *Visionary Women: Ecstatic Prophecy in Seventeenth-Century England*. Berkeley: University of California Press, 1995.

Manetta, Tony. "Fort Loudoun—Pennsylvania State Historic Site." *Clio: Your Guide to History* (blog), April 25, 2020. https://theclio.com/tour/2105/29.

Manning, M. Chris. "Magic, Religion, and Ritual in Historical Archaeology." *Historical Archaeology* 48, no. 3 (2014): 1–9.

———. "The Material Culture of Ritual Concealments in the United States." *Historical Archaeology* 48, no. 3 (2014): 52–83.

Mather, Cotton. *Magnalia Christi Americana: Or, the Ecclesiastical History of New-England: From Its First Planting in the Year 1620. Unto the Year of Our Lord, 1698. In Seven Books...By...Cotton Mather.* Vol. 2. London: Thomas Parkhurst, 1853.

McLaurin, Banks. *Descendants of Barnabas Horton of Southold, Compiled by Banks McLaurin Jr., on the Occasion of the Horton Reunion, Southold, New York, Sept 28-30, 1990, in Honor of the 350th Anniversary of the Founding of Southold, A.D. 1640.* Dallas, TX, 1990.

McMillan, Timothy J. "Black Magic: Witchcraft, Race, and Resistance in Colonial New England." *Journal of Black Studies* 25, no. 1 (1994): 99–117.

Minutes of the Executive Council of the Province of New York (Albany, NY 191), Vol. 2.

Moerman, Daniel E. *Native American Food Plants: An Ethnobotanical Dictionary.* Portland, OR: Timber Press, 2010.

Morris, Ira K. *Morris's Memorial History of Staten Island, New York.* Vol. 2. Staten Island, NY: Winthrop Press, 1900.

Moyer, Paul B. *Detestable and Wicked Arts: New England and Witchcraft in the Early Modern Atlantic World.* Ithaca, NY: Cornell University Press, 2020.

Norton, Mary Beth. *In the Devil's Snare: The Salem Witchcraft Crisis of 1692.* New York: Vintage, 2002.

O'Callaghan, Edmund Bailey. *Documents Relative to the Colonial History of the State of New-York.* Edited by Berthold Fernow. 15 vols. Albany, NY: Weed, Parsons, and Company, 1853–61.

———. "1850 Trial for Witchcraft." In *The Documentary History of the State of New York.* Vol. 4, 85–85. Albany, NY: Weed and Parsons, 1850.

Occum, Samson. "An Account of the Montauk Indians." *Massachusetts Historical Society, Collections* 1, no. 10 (n.d.): 107.

Onion, Daniel K. "Corn in the Culture of the Mohawk Iroquois." *Economic Botany*, 1964.

Orion, Loretta. *It Were as Well to Please the Devil as Anger Him: Witchcraft in the Founding Days of East Hampton.* CreateSpace Independent Publishing Platform, 2018.

Ostrander, Emmett, and Vinton P. Ostrander. *Ostrander: A Genealogical Record 1660–1995.* Ostrander Family Assn. Marceline, MO: Walsworth Publishing Company, 1999.

Paltsits, Victor Hugo (Editor). *Minutes of the Executive Council of the Province of New York*, Vol. 2. Albany, NY: J. B. Lyon Company, State Printers. 1910.

Patchogue (Town Clerk). *Records of the Town of Brookhaven up to 1800.* Patchogue, NY: Office of the Advance, 1880.

"Patent. Cornelis Melyn; Staten Island, Except So Much as Has Already Been Granted to David Pietersen de Vries for a Bouwery." New York State Archives. Series A1880. Volume GG.

Peckham, Harriett C., and Waite Van Buren. *History of Cornelis Maessen Van Buren.* New York: Tobias A. Wright Printer and Publisher, 1913.

Pelletreau, William S. *Abstracts of Wills on File in the Surrogate's Office, City of New York (1655–1707).* Vol. 1. Collections of the New York Historical Society, 1892.

Perrine, Howland Delano. *The Wright Family of Oyster Bay Long Island, with the Ancestry of and Descent from Peter Wright and Nicholas Wright, 1423–1923.* New York, 1923.

Piwonka, Rutha. "The Lutheran Presence in New Netherland." *De Halve Maen* 60, no. 1 (1987): 1–4.

Pócs, Éva. *Between the Living and the Dead: A Perspective on Witches and Seers in the Early Modern Age.* Budapest: Central European University Press, 1998.

Porterfield, Amanda. *Female Piety in Puritan New England: The Emergence of Religious Humanism.* New York: Oxford University Press, 1992.

———. "Witchcraft and the Colonization of Algonquian and Iroquois Cultures." *Religion and American Culture* 2, no. 1 (1992): 103–24.

Pulsipher, David, ed. *Records of the Colony of New Plymouth in New England (New Plymouth Records).* Boston: Press of William White, 1859.

Ranlet, Philip. "A Safe Haven for Witches? Colonial New York's Politics and Relations with New England in the 1690s." *New York History* 90, no. 1/2 (2009): 37–57.

Ray, Benjamin C. *Satan and Salem: The Witch-Hunt Crisis of 1692.* Charlottesville: University of Virginia Press, 2015.

Records of the Particular Court of Connecticut, 1639–1663. Collections of the Connecticut Historical Society, Connecticut Historical Society, Hartford.

Reis, Elizabeth. *Damned Women: Sinners and Witches in Puritan New England.* Ithaca, NY: Cornell University Press, 1997.

Riddell, William Renwick. "Witchcraft in Old New York." *Journal of Criminal Law and Criminology* 19, no. 2 (1928): 252–58.

Rine, Holly Anne. "Intercultural Contact and the Creation of Albany's New Diplomatic Landscape, 1647–1680." PhD dissertation, University of New Hampshire, 2004.

Rogers, Horatio. *Mary Dyer of Rhode Island: The Quaker Martyr That Was Hanged on Boston Common, June 1, 1660.* Providence, RI: Preston and Rounds, 1896.

Rosaldo, Michelle Zimbalist. "Women, Culture, and Society: A Theoretical Overview." In *Woman, Culture, and Society*, edited by Michelle Zimbalist Rosaldo and Louise Lamphere, 17–42. Stanford, CA: Stanford University Press, 1974.

Schlosser, S.E. *Spooky New York: Tales of Hauntings, Strange Happenings, and Other Local Lore.* Guilford, CT: Globe Pequot Press, 2005.

Scott, Martin J. *Isaac Jogues: Missioner and Martyr.* New York: P.J. Kenedy & Sons, 1927.

Seaver, James E. *A Narrative of the Life of Mrs. Mary Jemison.* London: Howden, 1826.

Sewel, William. *The History of the Rise, Increase, and Progress of the Christian People Called Quakers, Intermixed with Several Remarkable Occurrences.* Vol. 1. Philadelphia: Friends Book Store, 1856.

Sheppard, Walter Lee, Jr. "Origin of the Bowers, Leeks and Crosthwaits of South Jersey." *American Genealogist* 26 (1950): 211.

Shorto, Russell. *The Island at the Center of the World.* New York: Vintage, 2005.

Siminoff, Faren R. *Crossing the Sound.* New York: New York University Press, 2004.

Skinner, Charles M. *Myths and Legends of Our Own Land.* New York: Start Classics Publishing, 2013.

Smith, Erminnie A. *Myths of the Iroquois 1880–1881.* Washington, D.C.: Government Printing Office, 1883.

Speck, Frank G. "Shamanism." In *Languages and Lore of the Long Island Indians*, edited by Gaynell Stone. Stony Brook, NY: Suffolk County Archaeological Association, 2016.

Spencer-Molloy, Frank. "Science Casts New Light on Witch Tale." *Hartford Courant*, October 31, 1993.

Stansbury, Jill. *Herbal Formularies for Health Professionals.* Vol. 1. *Digestion and Elimination, Including Gastrointestinal System, Liver and Gallbladder, Urinary System, and the Skin.* White River Junction, VT: Chelsea Green Publishing, 2018.

Steiner, Walter Ralph. *History of Medicine [in Connecticut].* Hartford, CT: States History Company, 1925.

Stone, Gaynell. "Rites and Customs: Healing Practices-Herbal Lore." In *Languages and Lore of the Long Island Indians.* Stony Brook, NY: Suffolk County Archaeological Association, 2016.

Strong, John. "Book Review of Belle Barstow. Setauket, Alias Brookhaven: The Birth of a Long Island Town with Chronological Records 1655–1679. New York: Author-House, 2004. Index, Bibliography, Pp. 631." *Long Island Historical Journal* 17, no. 1–2 (2004): 237–41.

———. "The Thirteen Tribes of Long Island: The History of a Myth." *Hudson Valley Regional Review* 9, no. 2 (1992): 39–73.

———. "Wyandanch: Sachem of the Montauks." In *Northeastern Indian Lives 1632–1816*, edited by Robert Grumet, 48–73. Amherst: University of Massachusetts Press, 1996.

Taylor, John Metcalf. *The Witchcraft Delusion in Colonial Connecticut, 1647–1697.* New York: Grafton Press, 1908.

Thatcher, B.B. *Indian Biography: Or, an Historical Account of Those Individuals Who Have Been Distinguished among the North American Natives as Orators, Warriors, Statesmen, and Other Remarkable Characters.* New York: Harper and Brothers, 1836.

Thompson, Benjamin F. *The History of Long Island from Its Discovery and Settlement, to the Present Time. With Many Important and Interesting Matters; Including Notices of Numerous Individuals and Families; Also a Particular Account of the Different Churches and Ministers.* Vol. 1. 2nd ed. New York: Gould Banks & Co., 1843.

Thompson, Harold W. *Body, Boots, and Britches: Folktales, Ballads and Speech from Country New York.* Syracuse, NY: Syracuse University Press, 1979.

Thurston, Robert W. *Witch, Wicce, Mother Goose: The Rise and Fall of the Witch Hunts in Europe and North America.* Edinburgh: Longman, 2001.

Thwaites, Reuben Gold, ed. *The Jesuit Relations and Allied Documents: Travels and Explorations of the Jesuit Missionaries in New France, 1610–1791.* 73 vols. Cleveland, OH: Burrows Brothers, 1896.

Tooker, William Wallace. *Indian Place Names on Long Island.* Port Washington, NY: Ira J. Friedman, 1911.

Trumbull, J. Hammond, ed. *The Public Records of the Colony of Connecticut, Prior to the Union with New Haven Colony (May 1665)*. Hartford, CT: Brown and Parsons, 1850.

Upham, Charles Wentworth. *Salem Witchcraft: With an Account of Salem Village, and a History of Opinions on Witchcraft and Kindred Subjects*. Boston: Wiggin and Lunt Publishers, 1867.

Van Der Sijs, Nicoline. *Cookies, Coleslaw, and Stoops: The Influence of Dutch on the North American Languages*. Amsterdam University Press, 2009.

Van Laer, A.J.F. *Minutes of the Court of Albany, Rensselaerswyck and Schenectady 1680–1685*. Vol. 3. Albany: University of the State of New York, 1932.

Vecsey, Christopher. "The Story and Structure of the Iroquois Confederacy." *Journal of the American Academy of Religion* 54, no. 1 (1986): 79–106.

Walker, George Leon. *History of the First Church in Hartford, 1633–1883*. Hartford, CT: Brown & Gross, 1884.

Watson, Patricia A. *The Angelical Conjunction: The Preacher-Physicians of Colonial New England*. Knoxville: University of Tennessee Press, 1991.

Weeks, Archibald C. *Brookhaven Town Records 1662–1679*. Vol. 1. New York: Tobias A. Wright, 1924.

Weiser-Alexander, Kathy. "Witches of Massachusetts- C." *Legends of America* (blog), 2020. https://www.legendsofamerica.com/ma-witches-c/2/.

Wheeler, Walter Richard. "Magical Dwelling: Apotropaic Building Practices in the New World Dutch Cultural Hearth." In *Religion, Cults & Rituals in the Medieval Rural Environment*, edited by Christiane Bis-Worch and Claudia Theune, 373–96. Ruralia XI. Leiden: Sidestone Press, 2017.

Wilson, David. *The Life of Jane McCrea, with an Account of Burgoyne's Expedition in 1777*. New York, Baker, Goodwin & Company, 1853.

Winfield, Mason. *Shadows of the Western Door: Haunted Sites and Ancient Mysteries of Upstate New York*. Buffalo, NY: Western New York Wares, 1997.

Woodward, Walter W. *Prospero's America: John Winthrop, Jr., Alchemy, and the Creation of New England Culture, 1606–1676*. Chapel Hill: University of North Carolina Books, 2010.

———, trans. "The Trial of Katherine Harrison." *OAH Magazine of History* 17, no. 4 (2003): 37–56.

INDEX

ABOUT THE AUTHOR

S.R. Ferrara, MA RPA, was born and raised in Massapequa, New York, and grew up on oral traditions about local folklore, colonial history and the sea. He served two full combat deployments to the Helmand Province, Afghanistan, as a USMC infantry rifleman. After his honorable discharge, he promptly enrolled in college courses under the GI Bill with a need to understand culture and society. He has extensively traveled the world with his wife, Tara, learning about cultural fears of the supernatural and collecting ritual apotropaic items. Ferrara is a trained archaeobotanist and currently teaches courses at Queens College while he pursues his doctorate in anthropological archaeology at the Graduate Center, City University of New York. His research foci concern the archaeology of human plant use, colonialism in northeastern North America and community-based archaeology. However, his past excavations have taken him from Mayan pyramids in the jungles of Central America to scuba-assisted recovery operations of ancient Roman shipwrecks off the coast of Israel and contract archaeological work in the tristate area.